Introduction

Planning a practice that motivates kids to play, learn and enjoy the game of hockey is one of the most important responsibilities of a youth hockey coach. Hockey players want and need to be excited to participate and enthused while they learn. A player will benefit most from practices that are challenging, fun and well organized.

The Half Ice Drill Book has been written to provide coaches with a variety of half ice drills. Due to the need to increase shared ice practices, this book will become a valuable tool for a coach to use in their practice preparation. These drills are specifically designed to challenge players, to keep them active, interested and involved. These drills can also be easily adapted to a wide range of ages and abilities.

Legend

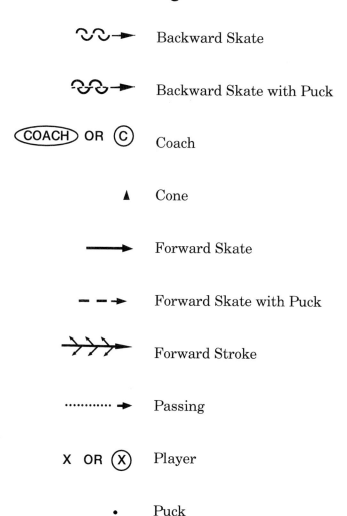

∽∽→   Backward Skate

ᴈᴈ→   Backward Skate with Puck

⟨COACH⟩ OR Ⓒ   Coach

▲   Cone

──→   Forward Skate

– – →   Forward Skate with Puck

⟫⟫⟫→   Forward Stroke

·········→   Passing

X OR Ⓧ   Player

•   Puck

⟹   Shooting

I I   Stopping

Dedication

This book is dedicated to the countless number of volunteers who have devoted their time and energy to the development of youth hockey. In giving of themselves, these volunteers have helped thousands of players develop their skills, realize their dreams and become better citizens. More importantly, they helped prepare these young athletes to meet life's greater challenges

SKATING DRILLS

Name: Four Lines

Objective: To develop better basic stride and balance in skating.

Age Group: Mites, Squirts

Organization of Drill: Players line up in equal lines behind the four cones along the goal line as shown. Players perform the exercise from the list provided under "Variations."

Teaching Points: Emphasis is based on the maneuver being performed.

Variations: All exercises are performed to the center line.

      a. Perform 4-single leg knee drops.
      b. Perform 3-double leg knee drops.
      c. Perform 2 belly flops.
      d. Perform two consecutive strides with the same leg.
      e. Perform small C inside edge strides.
      f. Perform big C inside edge cuts.

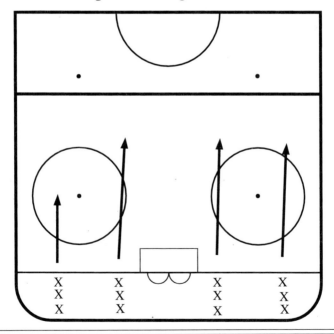

Name: Figure 8s

Objective: Improve skating; crossovers and agility.

Age Group: All

Organization of Drill: Players perform crossovers around the top half of the first end zone circle, then complete crossovers around the other end zone circle, then return to perform crossovers around the bottom of the original circle.

Teaching Points: Emphasize heel over toe when performing crossovers. With older, more accomplished groups, emphasize crossunder cuts with the inside leg.

Variations: · Perform skating backwards.
              · Perform skating with a puck.

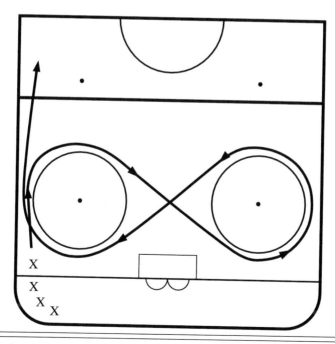

Name: Button Hook the Dots and Cones

Objective: To improve power turns.

Age Group: Mites, Pee Wees

Organization of Drill: Players skate in single file around each cone/dot, performing power turns at full speed.

Teaching Points: Emphasize keeping shoulders parallel with the ice and leaning on the outside edge of the inside skate. Encourage a crossunder as they come out of the turn.

Variations: Perform pivots around each cone/dot.

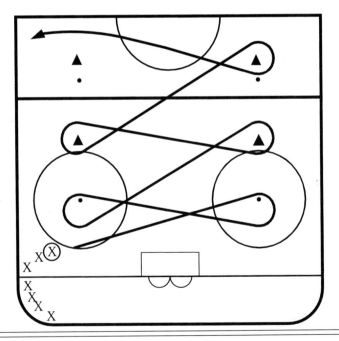

Name: Big S Drill

Objective: To improve power turns.

Age Group: Mites, Pee Wees

Organization of Drill: Players skate across the zone at the faceoff dots, blue line and center line, performing power turns.

Teaching Points: Emphasize keeping shoulders parallel with the ice and leaning on the outside edge of the inside skate. Encourage a crossunder as they come out of the turn.

Variations: Use your creativity.

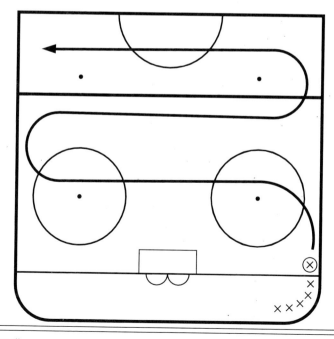

Name: Two Big Circles

Objective: To improve crossovers.

Age Group: Mites and Above

Organization of Drill: Players skate crossovers around the end zone faceoff circle in one direction, then perform another circle using crossovers while skating in the opposite direction.

Teaching Points: Emphasize keeping their feet moving, reaching in with each crossover step.

Variations: Perform the drill skating backwards.

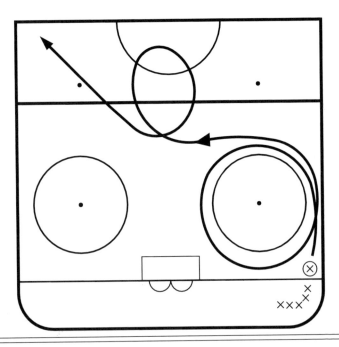

Name: The Big Skate

Objective: To improve crossovers.

Age Group: Mites and Above

Organization of Drill: Players skate hard up to the blue line, then perform crossovers back toward the end zone. They continue into the corner then perform crossovers and skate up the center line again.

Teaching Points: Emphasize keeping their feet moving, reaching in with each crossover step.

Variations: Perform the drill skating backwards.

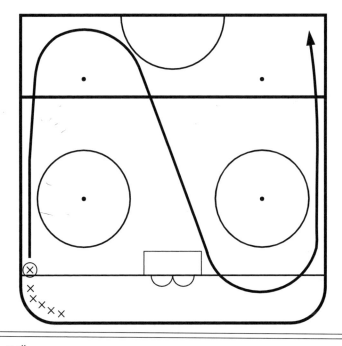

Name: Pivots Drill

Objective: To improve pivoting from forward to backward and backward to forward.

Age Group: Squirts and Above

Organization of Drill: Players line up just outside the blue line as shown. Each player then skates past each cone pivoting forward to backward or backward to forward, always facing toward the net.

Teaching Points: Emphasize keeping their feet moving.

Variations: Perform the drill carrying a puck.

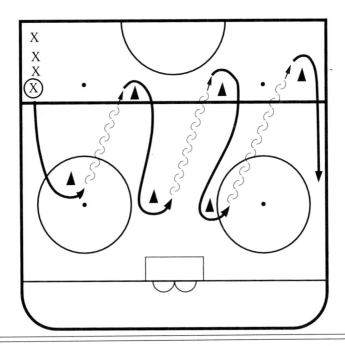

Name: Pivots on the Circle

Objective: To improve pivoting from forward to backward and backward to forward.

Age Group: Squirts and Above

Organization of Drill: Players line up just off the circle as shown. Each player then skates the circle and at each of the four compass points, pivots forward to backward then backward to forward, always facing up ice.

Teaching Points: Emphasize keeping their feet moving.

Variations: Perform the drill carrying a puck.

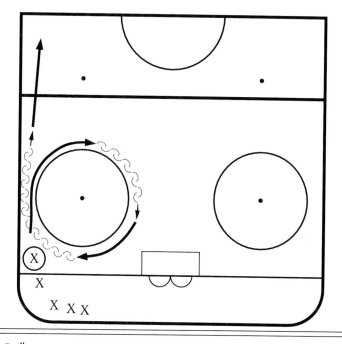

Name: Peanut

Objective: To improve skating; power turns.

Age Group: All

Organization of Drill: Players line up behind the first cone as shown, then skate through the cones performing power turns around each.

Teaching Points: Emphasize keeping shoulders parallel with the ice and leaning on the outside edge of the inside skate.

Variations: Perform the drill carrying a puck.

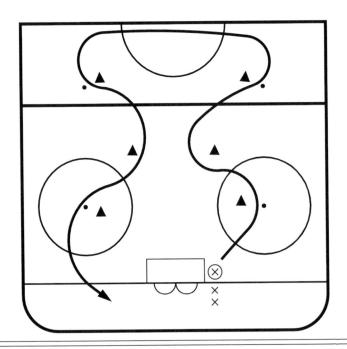

Name: Circles and Dots

Objective: To improve skating; crossovers and power turns.

Age Group: All

Organization of Drill: Players line up by the boards as shown. They perform crossovers around the end zone faceoff circle, a power turn around each of the neutral zone faceoff dots and crossovers around the other end zone faceoff circle.

Teaching Points: Emphasize keeping shoulders parallel with the ice and leaning on the outside edge of the inside skate; also emphasize a full crossover with a crossunder.

Variations: Perform the drill carrying a puck.

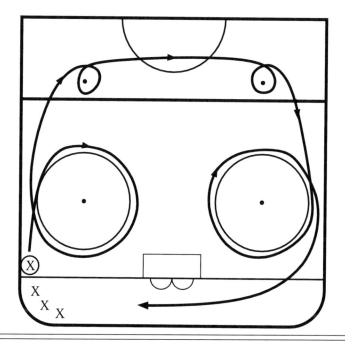

Name: Stops and Starts

Objective: To improve skating; stopping and returning.

Age Group: All

Organization of Drill: Place cones in the half ice area as shown. Player X skates around the first cone and then performs a stop, always facing up ice.

Teaching Points: Emphasize keeping shoulders parallel with the ice and pushing down hard into the ice in order to stop as quickly as possible.

Variations: Perform the drill carrying a puck.

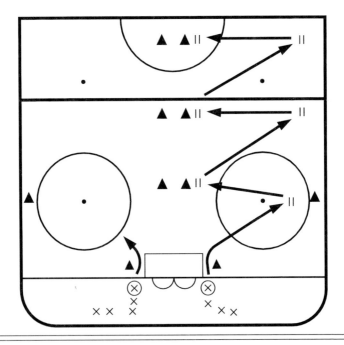

Name: Long W Drill

Objective: To improve skating; pivoting and skating backward.

Age Group: Squirts and Above

Organization of Drill: Players line up along the boards by the blue line. Each player performs 3-4 pivots between the blue and center lines then skates backward around the bottom of the end zone faceoff circle, pivots, and skates to the top of the other end zone faceoff circle.

Teaching Points: Emphasize keeping the head up and chest out. Use hard crossunders to pull yourself in the proper direction.

Variations: Perform the drill carrying a puck.

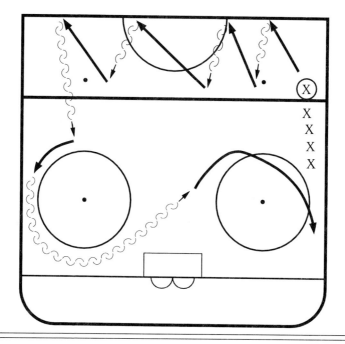

Name: Step Out Drill

Objective: To improve skating; pivoting and skating backwards.

Age Group: Squirts and Above

Organization of Drill: Players start the drill in the neutral zone, even with the inside edge of the faceoff circle. Players skate backward to the blue line, pivot and skate toward the boards. They pivot again and skate backward to the goal line. They skate forward around the net, pivot and skate backward until they are even with the faceoff dot. They pivot again and skate to the boards; then pivot again and skate backward to the center line, pivot, and go to the end of the line.

Teaching Points: Emphasize keeping the head up and chest out. Use hard crossunders to pull yourself in the proper direction.

Variations: Perform the drill carrying a puck.

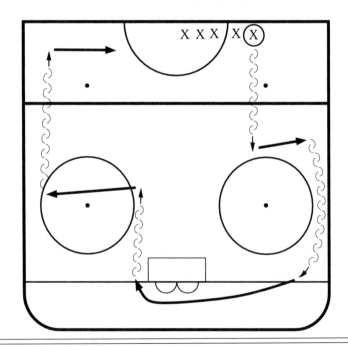

Name: All Out Drill

Objective: To improve overall skating.

Age Group: Squirts and Above

Organization of Drill: Players line up along the boards by the hash marks. Players start the drill by skating backward to the cone, pivoting and skating forward to the faceoff dot. There they perform a 360-degree spin around the dot, pivot at the blue line and skate backward to the bottom of the circle. They pivot at the bottom of the circle and perform crossovers around the rest of the circle before skating to the end of the line.

Teaching Points: Emphasize keeping the head up and chest out. Use hard crossunders to pull yourself in the proper direction.

Variations: Perform the drill starting on the opposite side.

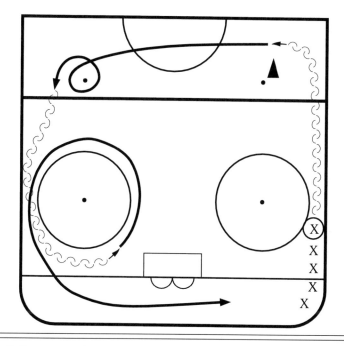

Name: Straight Line Skating

Objective: To improve stopping and starting skills. To train the player to always face the puck when stopping.

Age Group: Squirts and Above

Organization of Drill: Refer to the group on the left hash marks. Divide the players into groups of five (three may also be used). Player O2 starts with the puck with Xs lined up half way between O1 and O2, and O2 and O3. When O2 passes to O1, X1 confronts O1 while X2 moves to confront O2 to discourage the pass. The puck is then passed between the Os. The Xs confront but do not aggressively attack the puck carrier. They always stop and start facing the Os.

Teaching Points: Emphasize quick starting and stopping; no crossovers when changing directions.

Variations: Perform the drill in various areas on the ice (as shown).

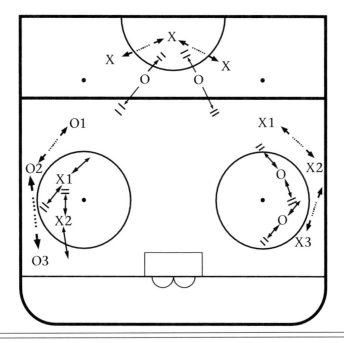

PUCKHANDLING DRILLS

Name: Two Cone Drive Skate

Objective: To improve deking and drive-skating technique.

Age Group: All

Organization of Drill: Players line up as shown, and take turns attacking the net. Players perform a deke on the first cone to the inside, then a fake to the outside on the second cone. The player should then drive to the middle to get a good shooting angle before he/she shoots.

Teaching Points: Emphasize a good deke at each cone and hard drive-skating after the second deke.

Variations: Be sure players alternate sides after performing the drill each time.

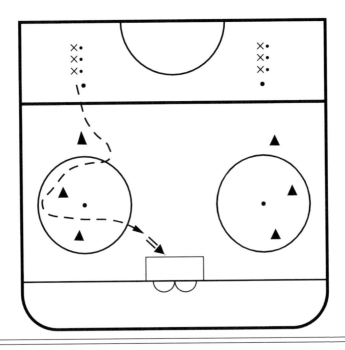

Name: Drive Skate Against a Coach

Objective: To improve puck protection technique.

Age Group: All

Organization of Drill: In the drill on the left, players skate around the circle and use good puck protection technique to prevent the coach from poking the puck away. In the drill on the right, the player drive-skates around the coach.

Teaching Points: Emphasize using speed and the body to protect the puck from an attacker.

Variations: The coach should use varying degrees of pressure based on the puckhandling skill of the individual player.

Name: Three Across Drills

Objective: To improve puckhandling technique.

Age Group: All

Organization of Drill: Players divide into groups of threes to perform the drill. The players then alternate, performing the assigned puckhandling technique(s).

Teaching Points: Emphasize exaggerating each deke.

Variations: a. Straight ahead skating at full speed.
b. Dekes to the right and left.
c. Puckhandle to center and make a quick pass after a deke to the next player.

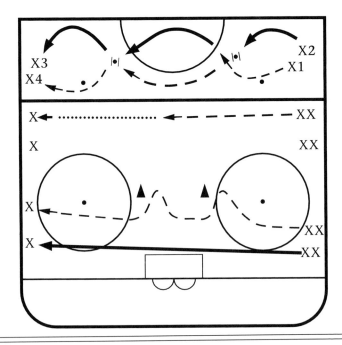

Name: Three Cone Deking Drill

Objective: To improve puckhandling technique.

Age Group: All

Organization of Drill: Players divide into two groups and line up as shown. Players alternate, performing dekes to the outside on each cone. After the last deke the player skates in and takes a shot on net, moving to the other line.

Teaching Points: Emphasize exaggerating each deke.

Variations: Place a coach or player to make passive or aggressive pokes at the puck as the players skate by.

Name: Keep Away in a Circle

Objective: To develop puckhandling and puck protection techniques.

Age Group: All

Organization of Drill: Players are divided into partners and alternate playing one-on-one against each other in a faceoff circle. Players work for 30 seconds and then are replaced by a new pair of skaters.

Teaching Points: Maintaining control of the puck. No overly aggressive play.

Variations: One player may be asked to turn his/her stick around and play defensively for the 30 second period.

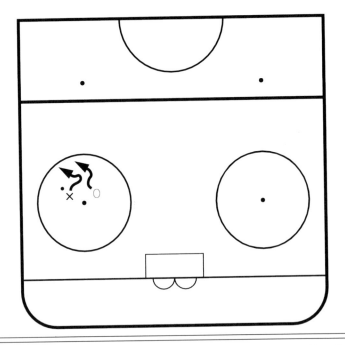

Name: One-on-One Puck Protection

Objective: To improve puck protection technique.

Age Group: Squirts and Above

Organization of Drill: Players line up on the side boards and at the faceoff dot. X1 tries to carry the puck behind the net. Should X2 cut him/her off, X1 performs an escape and turns away from the check protecting the puck with his/her body, before turning up ice.

Teaching Points: Have X1 skate hard and try to beat X2 to the other side of the ice before trying to escape.

Variations: Move the starting points of X1 and X2 to make it easier or more difficult for X1 to succeed.

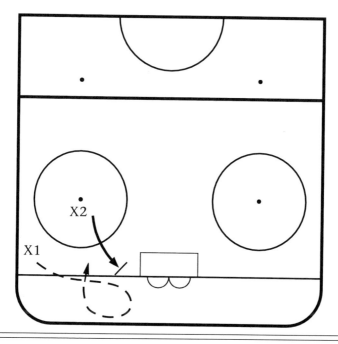

Name: Through the Checkers

Objective: To improve puckhandling and one-on-one techniques.

Age Group: Squirts and Above

Organization of Drill: Players line up as shown with three players stationed between two cones set about 10 feet apart. The puck carriers try to skate between the cones while maintaining control of the puck.

Teaching Points: Use speed and puckhandling skills to beat the checkers.

Variations: Use coaches as the checkers. Take the sticks away from the checkers.

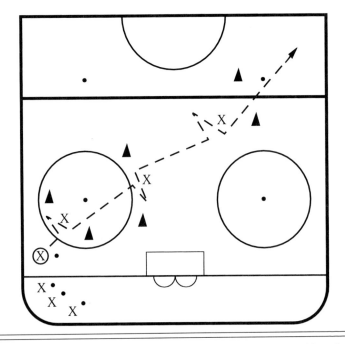

Name: Through the Checkers

Objective: To improve puckhandling and one-on-one techniques.

Age Group: Squirts and Above

Organization of Drill: Players line up as shown with three players stationed between two cones set about 10 feet apart. The puck carriers try to skate between the cones while maintaining control of the puck.

Teaching Points: Use speed and puckhandling skills to beat the checkers.

Variations: Use coaches as the checkers. Take the sticks away from the checkers.

Name: Across the Current

Objective: To improve puckhandling; keeping head and eyes up.

Age Group: Squirts and Above

Organization of Drill: Players line up as shown along the side boards and the goal line. On the whistle they skate across the zone and try to maintain control of their own puck. They can also try to poke other players' pucks away.

Teaching Points: Keep your head up and use a quick stick.

Variations: Use coaches as the checkers. Take the sticks away from the checkers.

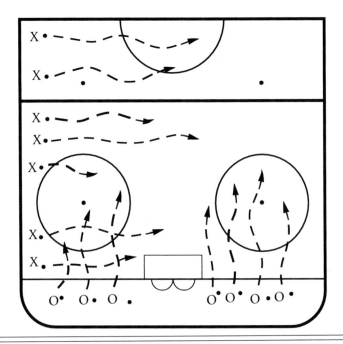

Name: Four Cone Rhythm Drill

Objective: To improve puckhandling rhythm.

Age Group: Squirts and Above

Organization of Drill: Players line up in two (or three) lines. Place cones about eight feet apart (the diagram shows the cones slightly farther apart). Players skate with the puck and slalom in and out of the cones.

Teaching Points: Shift your weight quickly and pull the puck to the bent knee.

Variations: Move the cones closer together as the players improve their skills.

Name: Change of Pace Drill

Objective: To improve change of pace skating, as well as read and react skills when being attacked by a forechecker.

Age Group: Squirts and Above

Organization of Drill: Players line up by the blue line as shown. X must skate behind the net, but then can continue to skate wide, cut back to the middle or reverse him/herself in order to avoid the checker.

Teaching Points: Use speed and deception to beat the checker.

Variations: Start the players from a different position or have them skate a different course.

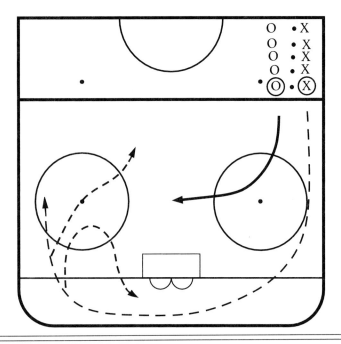

Name: Crossovers With a Deke

Objective: To improve speed while performing crossovers.

Age Group: Squirts and Above

Organization of Drill: Players line up in the center zone as shown. They perform dekes around each of the cones then skate hard crossovers.

Teaching Points: Exaggerate the dekes and skate hard.

Variations: Add a passive chaser to encourage faster skating, if necessary.

Name: Loop de Loop With a Stop

Objective: To improve puckhandling skill while maneuvering.

Age Group: Squirts and Above

Organization of Drill: Players line up by the hash marks. Players skate around the faceoff dot, skate hard to the net, stop, then skate around the other neutral zone faceoff dot and skate to the goal line again.

Teaching Points: Keep your feet moving.

Variations: Add a passive chaser to encourage faster skating.

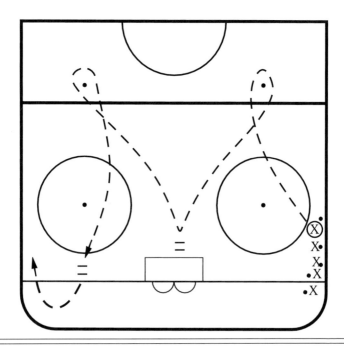

Name: Dekes With a Loop

Objective: To improve puckhandling skill while maneuvering.

Age Group: Squirts and Above

Organization of Drill: Players line up by the blue line. Players make a deke at each of the cones then skate hard through the end zone and perform crossovers (making a small circle) in the neutral zone.

Teaching Points: Keep your feet moving.

Variations: Add a passive chaser to encourage faster skating.

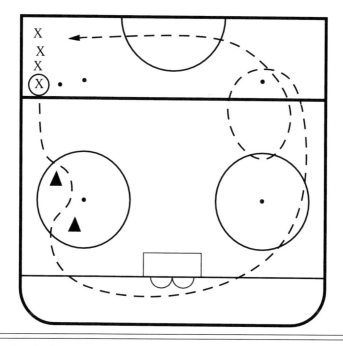

Name: Escapes on the Whistle

Objective: To improve puckhandling skill while maneuvering.

Age Group: Squirts and Above

Organization of Drill: Players begin the drill by skating around the half ice. Whenever the whistle blows, they perform an aggressive escape toward the boards, make two strides, then turn back toward the boards and continue skating.

Teaching Points: Keep your feet moving.

Variations: Skate the drill in both directions.

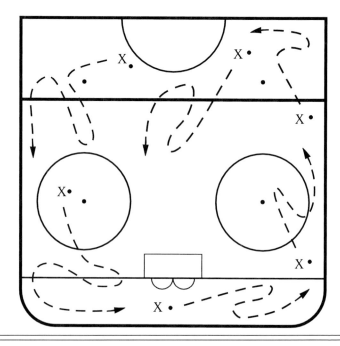

Name: Stops and Crossovers

Objective: To improve puckhandling skill while maneuvering.

Age Group: Squirts and Above

Organization of Drill: Players skate to each cone, stop, and quickly change directions. They then skate crossovers around the far end zone circle, skate around the net and perform crossovers going the opposite direction around the other end zone circle.

Teaching Points: Keep your feet moving.

Variations: Skate the drill in both directions.

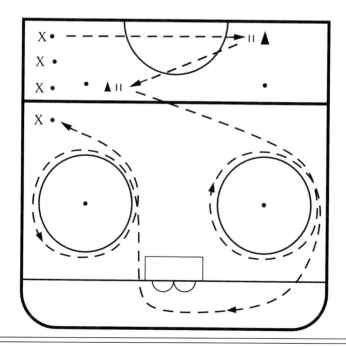

PASSING AND RECEIVING DRILLS

Name: Two-Man Passing

Objective: To develop good forehand and backhand passing techniques.

Age Group: Mites, Squirts, Pee Wees

Organization of Drill: Players develop two lines (as shown) and pass back and forth across the zone using forehand and backhand passes.

Teaching Points: Exaggerated passing and receiving techniques.

Variations: Have players perform drill skating backward (Pee Wees and Bantams).

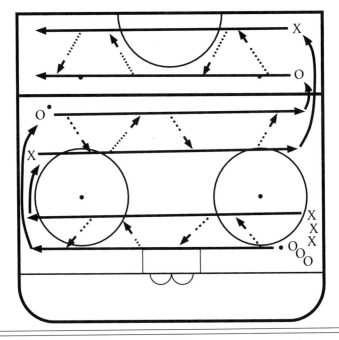

Name: Three-Man Follow Your Pass

Objective: To develop good forehand and backhand passing techniques. To develop the concept of give and go.

Age Group: Mites, Squirts, Pee Wees

Organization of Drill: Players line up on either side of the ice (as shown). The objective of the drill is to make a pass and then replace the person to whom you just passed. #3 and #6 move in and shoot on goal. #4 starts after #2 has made his/her pass.

Teaching Points: Exaggerate passing and receiving techniques.

Variations: Have players perform all passes on the backhand or receive all passes on the backhand.

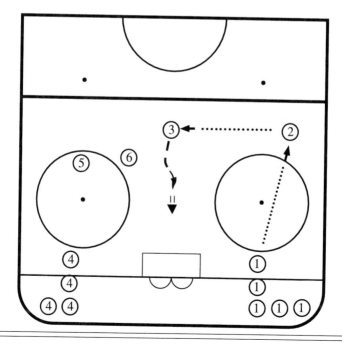

Name: Serpentine Skate With Stickhandling or Passing

Objective: To develop good maneuverability while stickhandling, passing and receiving.

Age Group: Squirts and Above

Organization of Drill: Players line up on either side of the ice. On the right, the first player in line skates around the cone, then to the second cone using crossovers before finishing by skating in and shooting. On the left, a pass is made to the next player in line at the blue line and then a return pass is made after the player reaches the blue line for the second time.

Teaching Points: Exaggerated passing and receiving techniques.

Variations: Use your creativity.

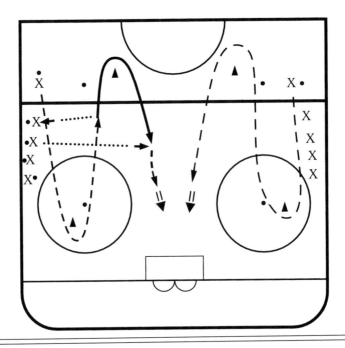

Name: Two-Man Pass and Shoot

Objective: To develop good stickhandling, passing and receiving.

Age Group: Squirts and Above

Organization of Drill: Players line up as shown. #1 starts out with a puck and shoots on net. He/she then picks up another puck behind the net and passes to #2 who, with timing, has broken around the top of the circle and then shoots on net.

Teaching Points: Emphasize the timing between #1 and #2.

Variations: Have #2 move behind the net and start the drill again by passing to the next #1 in line.

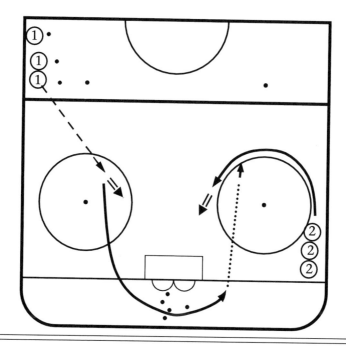

Name: Give and Go Into the Zone

Objective: To develop good stickhandling, passing and receiving.

Age Group: Squirts and Above

Organization of Drill: Players line up as shown. #1 starts out with a puck and passes to #2. #2 then returns the pass to #1 who shoots on goal. #3 and #4 then perform the same drill.

Teaching Points: Emphasize the timing between #1 and #2.

Variations: #1 or #2 could perform an escape before passing to each other.

Name: Give and Go With the Passer

Objective: To develop good stickhandling, passing and receiving.

Age Group: Squirts and Above

Organization of Drill: Players line up as shown. #2 starts out with a puck and passes to a coach or player, who makes a quick pass back to #2. #2 then goes in and shoots on net. #1 then performs the same drill.

Teaching Points: Show the passer where you want the puck by showing your stick and giving a target.

Variations: #1 or #2 could perform an escape before receiving the return pass.

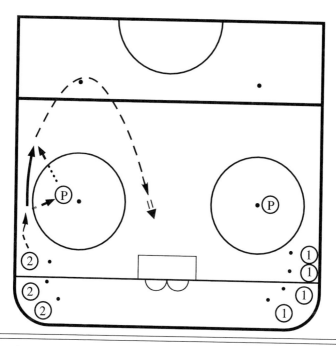

Name: Double Give and Go with the Passer

Objective: To develop good stickhandling, passing and receiving.

Age Group: Squirts and Above

Organization of Drill: Players line up as shown. #1 starts out and passes to the first passer with a quick give and go pass play. The first passer then makes a pass across the ice to the second passer to work another 'give and go. #1 then moves in after receiving a pass from the second passer and shoots on the net.

Teaching Points: Show the passer where you want the puck by showing your stick and giving a target.

Variations: Move the positions of passer #1 or #2.

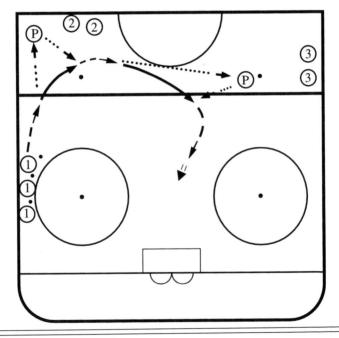

Name: Shooter With a Breakout Pass

Objective: To develop good stickhandling, passing and receiving.

Age Group: Squirts and Above

Organization of Drill: Players line up as shown. #1 starts out and takes a shot on net. He/she then picks up a puck and passes to #2, who has moved from the blue line to a breakout position along the boards. He/she then carries the puck to the blue line and passes to the next #1 in line.

Teaching Points: #2 should always have their chest on the puck.

Variations: Vary the location where #2 should receive the pass.

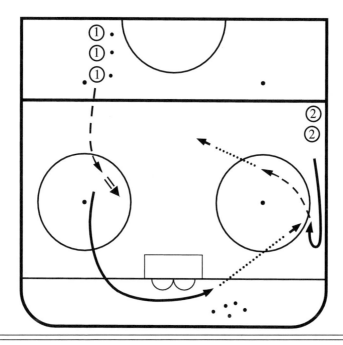

Name: Partner Passing With Variations

Objective: To develop good passing and receiving.

Age Group: Squirts and Above

Organization of Drill: Players line up in two sets of pairs and a set of three as shown. X1 and X2 alternate performing board passes to one another. X3 and X4 perform drop passes to one another. X5, X6 and X7 make short, quick passes as they stay in their lanes.

Teaching Points: Have X5, X6 and X7 perform one touch passes.

Variations: Use your creativity.

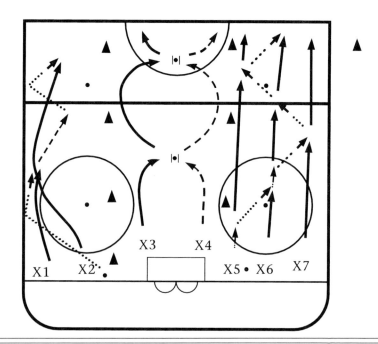

Name: Breakout Pass With a Board Pass

Objective: To develop good passing and receiving.

Age Group: Squirts and Above

Organization of Drill: Player #2 skates to the pucks and passes to #1 who has moved to a breakout position along the boards. #1 then makes a short board pass back to #2 who skates in and shoots on net. #3 and #4 perform the same drill on the opposite side.

Teaching Points: The board pass from #1 must be on an effective angle to reach #2.

Variations: Have #2 shoot on goal and then pick up a puck. Have a passive defender for #1 to make his/her board pass around.

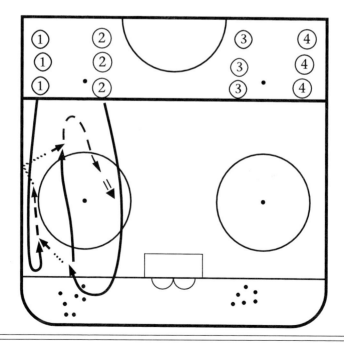

Name: 2 on 1 Get Open For a Pass

Objective: To develop the concept of skating off the puck and finding an opening so that the puck carrier can pass freely to an open player.

Age Group: Squirts and Above

Organization of Drill: On a circle or in a small area, two players try to maintain control of the puck. The puck carrier remains stationary. The defender tries to deny the pass to the player without the puck by shadowing him/her. Every time the pass is completed the drill pauses and the defender moves to the other player.

Teaching Points: The offensive player without the puck needs to use quick agility skating to get open. No passing through the defender.

Variations: With the same principles, play 3 vs. 2 defenders.

Name: Passing Square

Objective: To develop the concept of creating passing lanes for the puck carrier.

Age Group: Squirts and Above

Organization of Drill: Create a square using pylons or spray paint and start the drill as shown. As O1 passes to O3, O2 must move to one side of the square in order to provide a passing lane for O3 to pass to him/her. The passer should always have two passing options.

Teaching Points: It may take a few repetitions for the players to pick up this concept, but they will start moving instinctively in a short time.

Variations: Play 3 on 2 or 3 on 3 cross-ice games with the objective of maintaining control of the puck (no goals to shoot at).

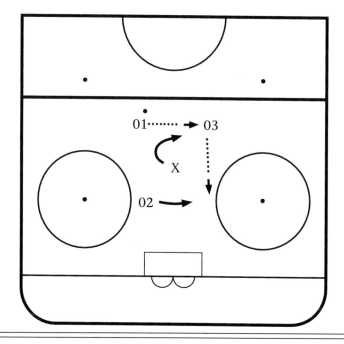

Name: Wide Pass/Short Pass

Objective: To develop quick, short passing and long, cross-ice passing skills.

Age Group: Squirts and Above

Organization of Drill: Players start out along the boards by the goal line as shown. X1 and X2 start by making long passes across the zone, then curl back toward the goal making short passes back and forth. Space the passers so they do not have too many skates to pass through.

Teaching Points: Remind players to stay in their lanes. No slap passing.

Variations: Variety with imagination.

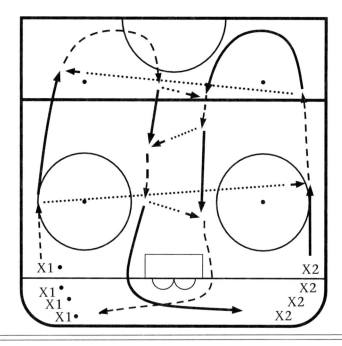

Name: Drop Pass Drill

Objective: To develop the concept of the drop pass on the attack.

Age Group: Squirts and Above

Organization of Drill: X1 and X2 line up as shown. X2 breaks and X1 passes to him/her. Both players skate a loop and meet at center ice, where X2 leaves a drop pass for X1. X1 carries the puck into the zone and can shoot or pass back to X2 for a shot.

Teaching Points: Call off-side infractions when they occur. Make sure the pass is a true drop pass and is not slid to X1.

Variations: Have X1 and X2 perform a skating maneuver, then resume the drop pass play.

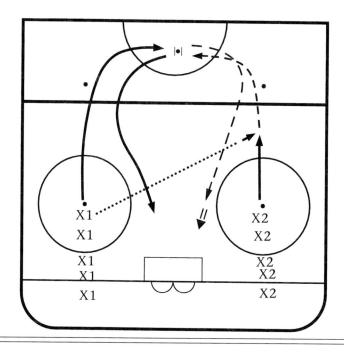

Name: Boston Two Pass Drill

Objective: Passing and receiving the puck on the move; timing your break to receive a pass.

Age Group: Pee Wees and Above

Organization of Drill: #1 and #2 line up as shown. #1 starts from the blue line even with the hash marks. He/She skates a wide arc down and then around the boards, making him/herself available for a pass. As the player turns up ice, the coach passes the puck. #2 starts his/her break and must time the break to receive the pass in stride while not looking back for it.

Teaching Points: Emphasize the timing of the play; sticks should remain on the ice as a target for the pass.

Variations: Have another player make the initial pass to #1. Have #2 curl and take a shot on goal. Start the drill by having #1 shoot on goal, then pick up a puck and make the pass to #2.

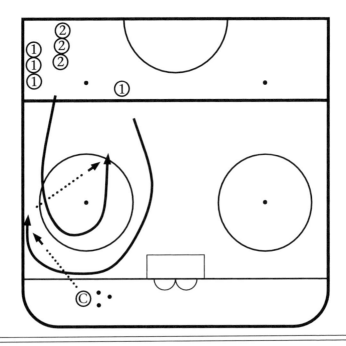

Name: Direct Pass/Board Pass Drill

Objective: Passing and receiving the puck on the move; timing your break to receive a pass; using the boards to make a pass.

Age Group: Pee Wees and Above

Organization of Drill: #1 and #2 line up as shown. #1 starts from the blue line even with the hash marks. He/She skates a wide arc down and then around the boards, making him/herself available for a pass. As the player turns up ice, the coach passes the puck. As #2 breaks across the zone, #1 must decide whether to make a direct pass or to use the boards for a pass.

Teaching Points: Emphasize the timing of the play; sticks should remain on the ice as a target for the pass.

Variations: Have another player make the initial pass to #1. Have #2 curl and take a shot on goal. Start the drill by having #1 shoot on goal, then pick up a puck and make the pass to #2.

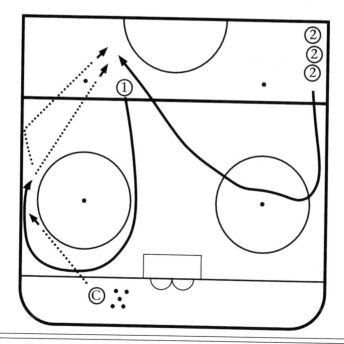

Name: Double Drop Pass Drill

Objective: To develop the concept of the drop pass on the attack.

Age Group: Squirts and Above

Organization of Drill: X1 and X2 line up as shown. X2 breaks and X1 passes to him/her. Both players skate a loop and meet at center ice, where X2 leaves a drop pass for X1. X1 and X2 loop again and perform a second drop pass. X2 can shoot or pass back to X1 for a shot.

Teaching Points: Call off-side infractions. Make sure both passes are true drop passes.

Variations: Use a double drop pass.

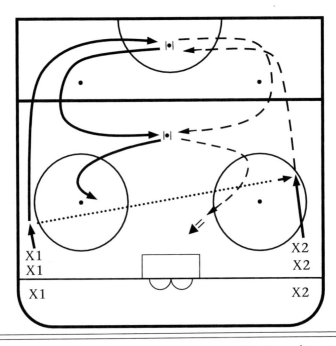

Name: Timing Drill

Objective: To develop the concept of timing.

Age Group: Squirts and Above

Organization of Drill: D and F skate across the zone. After passing the net, the defenseman must decide whether to make a direct pass or a board pass to F. If the pass fails, F should circle, making him/herself open for another pass. Meanwhile, D picks up another puck along the side boards and passes to F.

Teaching Points: Emphasize the concept of timing and getting open for a pass.

Variations:
- F could go in for a shot on net.
- F and D could play 1/1 back into the zone.

Name: Cycling Drill

Objective: To develop the concept of cycling in the offensive zone.

Age Group: Squirts and Above

Organization of Drill: #1s and #2s line up as shown. The first #1 lines up below the goal line with a puck, while #2 is at the blue line. #1 starts up the boards and bump passes the puck off the boards back toward the corner. #2 skates down the boards and continues skating into the corner, retrieves the puck and passes to #1 for a shot on net. #1 and #2 then change lines.

Teaching Points: Emphasize the concept of moving the puck to an open area to continue the attack.

Variations: Have #1 make a drop pass for #2. Add a passive or aggressive checker to the drill. Develop another cycling option.

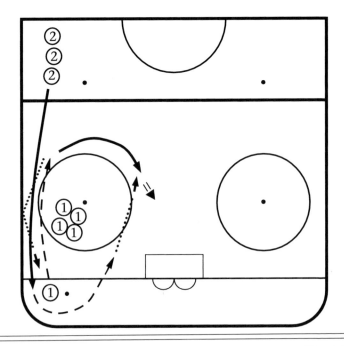

Name: Four Pass Drill

Objective: To develop passing skills in the context of a breakout.

Age Group: Squirts and Above

Organization of Drill: #1s, #2s, #3s and #4s line up as shown. The first #1 skates down past the cone and passes to #2. #2 then passes to #4, who in turn passes to #3, who has moved toward #4. #3 passes to #1, who has timed his/her break to receive a pass and then shoot on net. Rotate to the next line.

Teaching Points: Sharp, quick passes.

Variations: · Vary the positioning of the players.
· Add multiple tasks to the drill.

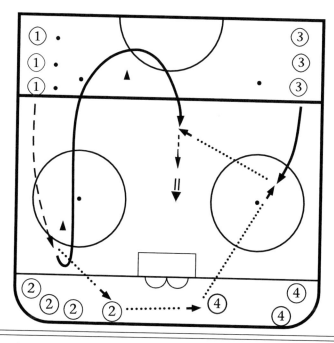

Name: Two Pass Drill

Objective: To develop passing and receiving skills.

Age Group: Squirts and Above

Organization of Drill: Station the line of Xs along the boards and station two passers as shown. X passes to P1, who then passes to P2, who returns a pass to X, who has skated out through the neutral zone and back toward the net. After receiving the pass, X shoots on net. Alternate the passers.

Teaching Points: Sharp, quick passes. X should be skating hard.

Variations: Vary the positioning and distances of the players.

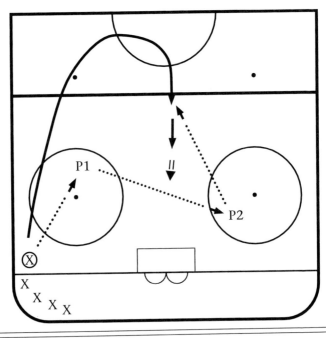

Passing and Receiving Drill

Name: Over and Back

Objective: To develop passing and receiving skills.

Age Group: Squirts and Above

Organization of Drill: Although one pair (X and O) are shown, as many as eight pairs of skaters can perform this drill at one time. X starts out skating backward with the puck while O skates toward him/her. As he/she nears the boards, X passes to O. X and O then alternate roles and continue to do so until the coach stops the drill.

Teaching Points: Sharp, quick passes. Moving the puck, not simply dragging it backward.

Variations: Have players skate forward with the puck, then pass it to their partner. Have the puck carrier perform a 360-degree spin before passing to his/her partner.

Name: Partners Give-and-Go

Objective: To develop passing and receiving skills, along with the concept of give-and-go passing.

Age Group: Squirts and Above

Organization of Drill: Players partner up and spread throughout the half ice area. They alternate making give-and-go passes to one another in a small area.

Teaching Points: Sharp, quick passes. Move to an open area after making each pass.

Variations: • Add a third player to try and deny the pass.
  • Add a second puck.

Name: Moran's Offensive Zone Passing Drill

Objective: To develop passing and receiving skills and the fake shot pass.

Age Group: Squirts and Above

Organization of Drill: Five players are lined up as shown with the rest of the team behind #1. #1-#4 pass the puck to the next person in line and then take their place for the next pass. When #5 gets the puck, he/she can shoot or, if the goaltender has cut down too much of the angle, can make a fake shot-pass to #4, who has moved to the side of the net.

Teaching Points: Sharp, quick passes.

Variations: · Have #5 move to a screen/deflecting spot after his/her turn shooting.
· Add another puck.

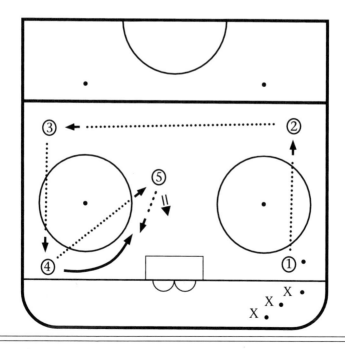

Name: Moran's Offensive Zone Passing Drill #2

Objective: To develop passing and receiving skills and the fake shot pass.

Age Group: Squirts and Above

Organization of Drill: Five players are lined up as shown with the rest of the team behind #1. #1-#4 pass the puck to the next person in line and then take their place for the next pass. When #5 gets the puck, he/she skates out of the corner and can shoot or, if the goaltender has cut down too much angle, can make a fake shot-pass to #4, who has moved to the side of the net.

Teaching Points: Sharp, quick passes.

Variations: Change the positioning of players #1-#3 before the attacking passes are made. Add additional tasks to the drill.

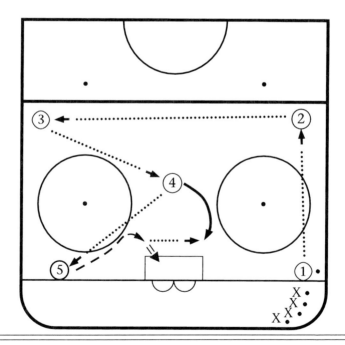

Name: Give-and-Go with a Pivot Drill

Objective: To develop quick passing and receiving skills with give-and-go concepts.

Age Group: Pee Wees and Above

Organization of Drill: Xs line up at the blue line as shown. The first X skates backward and receives a pass from the second player in line. These two players exchange three passes. X then pivots and skates backward to the center line, pivots and skates toward the net, and then receives a final return pass from his/her partner. X then attacks the net.

Teaching Points: Passes must be made quickly and accurately.

Variations: Reduce the number of passes for players with less-developed passing skills. Add additional tasks (i.e., tumbles, knee drops, etc.).

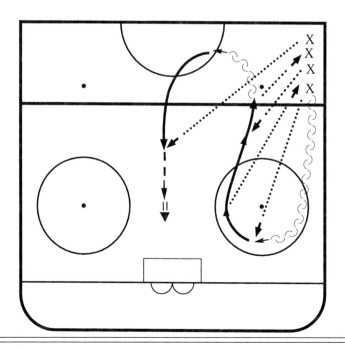

Name: Quick Give-and-Go with a Pivot Drill

Objective: To develop quick passing and receiving skills, along with give-and-go concepts.

Age Group: Squirts and Above

Organization of Drill: Xs line up at the blue line as shown. The first X skates backward and receives a pass from the second player in line. These two players exchange a give-and-go. X then pivots and skates backward to the center line, pivots and attacks the net.

Teaching Points: Passes must be made quickly and accurately.

Variations: Reduce the number of passes for players with less-developed passing skills.

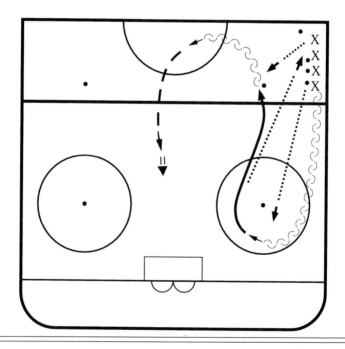

Name: Long Give-and-Go Pass Drill

Objective: To develop passing and receiving skills, along with give-and-go concepts.

Age Group: Squirts and Above

Organization of Drill: Xs and Os line up along the goal line as shown. The first X is positioned just inside the faceoff dot. On the whistle, he/she performs hard crossovers around the dot and receives a pass from the first O in line. He/She skates to the neutral zone, then turns back towards the net. O moves to just inside the faceoff dot. X and O then perform a give-and-go play with X shooting on net. O then starts the drill again.

Teaching Points: Passes must be made quickly and accurately.

Variations: Keep the lines closer for players with less-developed passing skills.

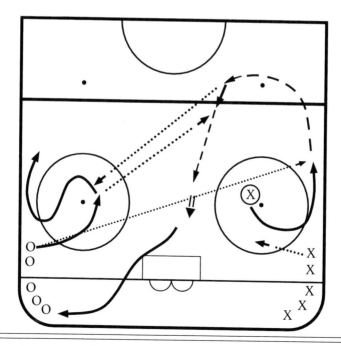

SHOOTING DRILLS

Name: Board Banger

Objective: To work on shooting skills.

Age Group: Mites, Squirts

Organization of Drill: Players line up along the boards in the neutral zone as shown, each with a puck. The player skates to center, takes a hard shot at the boards angling the puck towards the defensive zone. The player then picks up the puck and shoots on net.

Teaching Points: Shoot hard. Hit the net.

Variations: The players could perform dome skating maneuver before shooting the puck.

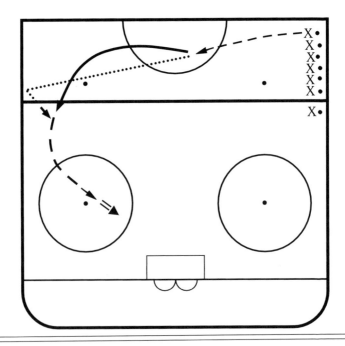

Name: Three Shot Drill

Objective: To develop shooting skills.

Age Group: Squirts and Above

Organization of Drill: Player X is located as shown and 2 shooting spots are designated with cones. X receives a pass from the coach and shoots on net. He/She then moves to position #2 and receives a pass from the other coach and shoots. X then returns to the first spot where he/she takes a third shot on net. The next player then steps into perform the drill.

Teaching Points: Give a target with your stick. Shoot for the openings. Shoot hard. Hit the net.

Variations: Vary the positions of the cones.

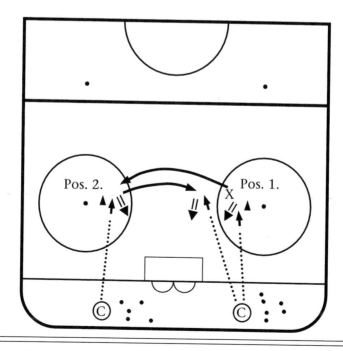

Name: Mancini

Objective: To develop shooting and deflecting skills.

Age Group: Squirts and Above

Organization of Drill: Players 1-5 are situated as shown. #2 passes to #1 and he/she shoots on net. Player #3 shoots and #1 tips and/or rebounds the shot. Player #4 shoots and #1 tips and/or rebounds the shot. Player #5 passes to #1 and he/she shoots on net. Players rotate positions and resume the drill.

Teaching Points: Good passes, shoot for the openings, jump on rebounds. Keep the puck on the ice.

Variations: Vary the shooting or passing positions.

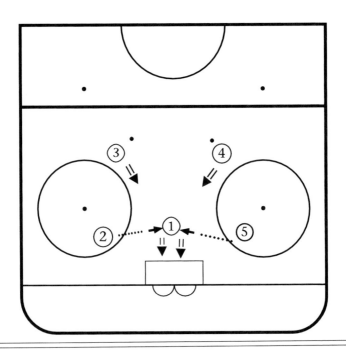

Name: Forehand/Backhand Shooting

Objective: To develop shooting on the forehand and backhand.

Age Group: Mites and Above

Organization of Drill: Players are lined up as shown. The first player in line skates with a puck around the circle and takes a shot on goal. The player then picks up a puck in the corner, skates around the circle and takes another shot on goal using the backhand shot if he/she had taken a forehand shot before (and visa versa).

Teaching Points: Hit the net.

Variations: After the player shoots, he/she screens for the next shooter.

Name: Point Shot, Tip/Deflect Drill

Objective: To develop tipping, screening and deflecting skills.

Age Group: Squirts and Above

Organization of Drill: Players are lined up as shown. X1 with a puck passes to D1 and moves to the front of the net. D1 shoots on net. X2 then performs the same drill.

Teaching Points: X1 should face the shooter with his/her stick on the ice. Shooter keep the puck on the ice.

Variations: X2 passes to D2, then moves to the front of the net.

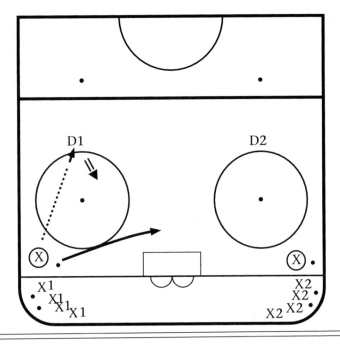

Name: Slot Shot Drill

Objective: To develop accurate shooting and quick release after a pass.

Age Group: Squirts and Above

Organization of Drill: Players are lined up as shown. X1 with a puck passes to X3 who shoots on net. X2 immediately passes to X3 who takes another shot on net. Players then move to the next position in line.

Teaching Points: X3 should be sure to show the passer with his/her stick where they want the pass.

Variations: X3 screens for the next shooter.

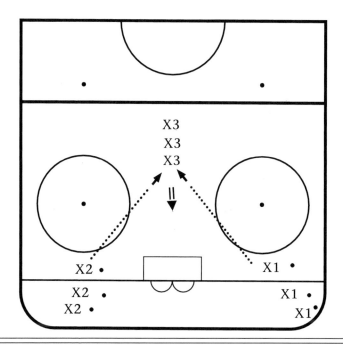

Name: Shooting on the Fly Drill

Objective: To develop accurate shooting and quick release after a pass. To shoot before the goaltender can cut the angle.

Age Group: Squirts and Above

Organization of Drill: Players line up as shown. O passes puck to player who has broken for the net. X shoots the puck immediately at the net.

Teaching Points: X should be sure to show the passer with his/her stick where they want the pass.

Variations: X screens for the next shooter. X can make a quick pass back to O and move to the net for a tip or screen opportunity.

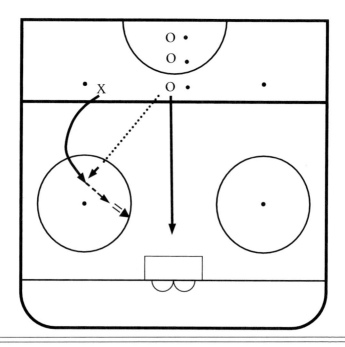

Name: Goal Mouth Tip Drill

Objective: To develop the ability to score from a goal mouth pass.

Age Group: Squirts and Above

Organization of Drill: Players are lined up as shown. X with a puck carries the puck deep and then passes to O at the goal mouth.

Teaching Points: O should be sure to show the passer with his/her stick where they want the pass. O should place more pressure on the stick blade to ensure that the puck does not come off the stick and into the corner.

Variations: Be sure all players rotate to each position.

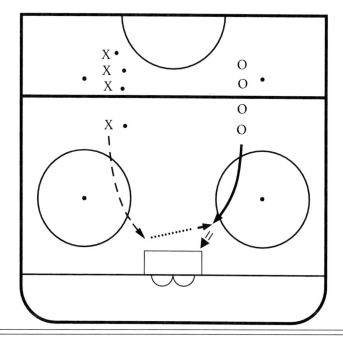

Name: Find an Open Lane Drill

Objective: To develop the ability to get open to receive a pass in the slot area.

Age Group: Squirts and Above

Organization of Drill: Players are lined up as shown. X1 with a puck, and X2 his/her partner move towards the goal (X1 must remain below the goal line). X2 must find a spot where X1 can pass to him/her. (Note: cones area scattered around the zone).

Teaching Points: The coach should identify that timing and having the stick on the ice are important to helping the puck carrier get the puck to them successfully.

Variations: Be sure all players rotate to each position.

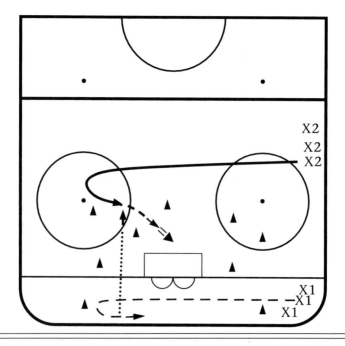

Name: Three Shot Drill

Objective: To develop quick release after receiving a pass.

Age Group: Squirts and Above

Organization of Drill: Players are lined up as shown. X receives a pass from #1 and shoots on net. #2 then passes immediately to X for a second shot; #3 follows #2 doing the same. Be sure all players rotate to each position.

Teaching Points: The coach should identify that having the stick on the ice with the proper angle is important to helping receive the puck and get a shot off quickly.

Variations: Vary the positions of the passers. Also can add multiple tasks to the drill.

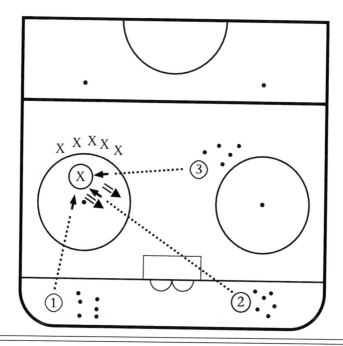

Name: Two Shot Drill

Objective: To develop backwards skating with the puck and quick release after receiving a pass.

Age Group: Squirts and Above

Organization of Drill: Players are positioned as shown and each has a puck. #1 skates backwards with a puck to the top of the circles, stops and shoots. #2 then performs the same drill. As #2 performs the drill, #1 skates towards his/her line and gets a pass from the next #1 in line. He/she then passes to #2 for a second shot as soon as he/she is ready to receive the pass.

Teaching Points: Coaches need to remind the players that they must time their passes.

Variations: Vary the skating maneuvers that the players perform before they make their shots and passes.

Name: 2 on 2 Get Open Drill

Objective: To train players to read and react, and to be able to move to open ice for a pass.

Age Group: Squirts and Above

Organization of Drill: Players are positioned as shown. #1 may skate anywhere behind the goal line with a puck. #2 and #3 must try to get away from the checkers, the Xs. Allow 10-30 seconds of play and then rotate players.

Teaching Points: Coaches need to remind the players to work hard and execute good passes.

Variations: Add more checkers and offensive players.

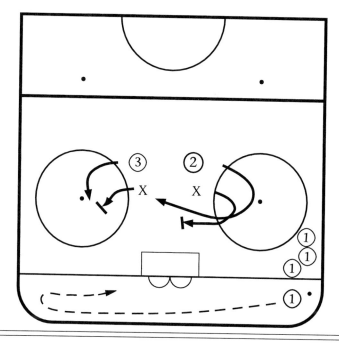

Name: Arc and Pass Drill

Objective: To train players to maintain the attack after the shot has been taken.

Age Group: Squirts and Above

Organization of Drill: Players are positioned as shown. #1 skates around the circle and receives a pass from the second player in line. After shooting, he/she picks up a puck below the goal line and passes to the next player in line who has arced across the top of the circle. When all the players on this side have gone, the #2s perform the same drill.

Teaching Points: Remind players to time their break with the passer in the corner.

Variations: Have the passer move to the net for a rebound after making the pass.

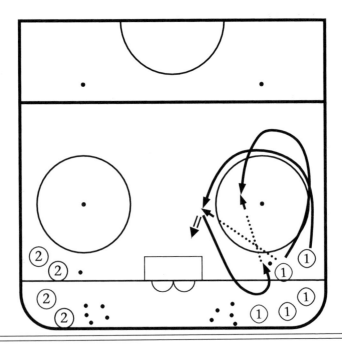

Name: Shoot and Tip Drill

Objective: To teach players to maintain the attack after shooting. To improve scoring ability around the net.

Age Group: Squirts and Above

Organization of Drill: Players are positioned as shown. #1 skates in with a puck and shoots on net. He/she then breaks towards the net and receives a goal mouth pass from #2 in the corner.

Teaching Points: Remind players that when tipping a pass, the should place extra weight on the blade of the stick with the bottom hand.

Variations: Position the passer behind the net.

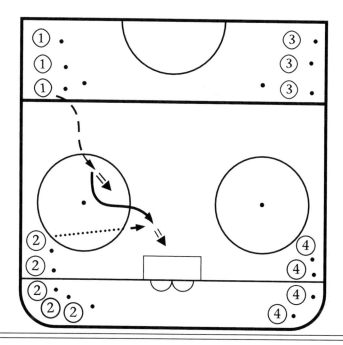

Name: Pivot and Shoot Drill

Objective: To teach players to maintain the attack after the shot. To improve scoring ability around the net.

Age Group: Mites and Above

Organization of Drill: Position the players as shown. The first X in line skates backwards across the blue line. He/she drops the blade of his/her stick to the ice when wanting to receive a pass from the second player in line. He/she then pivots and shoots on net.

Teaching Points: Place your stick on the ice to signal the passer that you are ready for the pass.

Variations: Add a knee drop to the drill performed after making the pivot and before shooting.

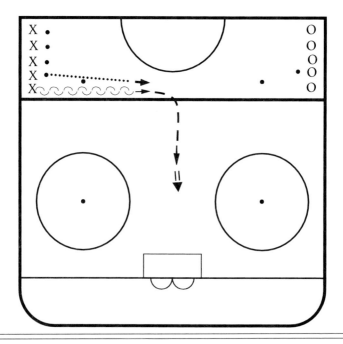

Name: Tight Crossovers and Shoot Drill

Objective: To develop quickness and shooting skills, while skating at full speed.

Age Group: Mites and Above

Organization of Drill: Position players as shown. The first #1 in line skates a tight crossover around the face-off dot in the neutral zone and attacks the net.

Teaching Points: Encourage players to skate around the puck as they make their crossovers. Remind them to accelerate coming out of their crossovers as they head to the net.

Variations: Add a knee drop to the drill performed after making the pivot and before shooting.

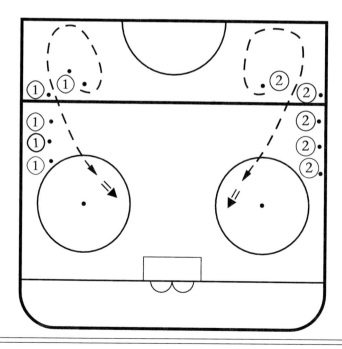

Name: Double Slot Shot Drill

Objective: To develop scoring ability from the slot area.

Age Group: Squirts and Above

Organization of Drill: Xs and Os line up in the corners as shown. The first X skates to the slot and receives a pass from the first O in line and shoots immediately. He/she performs a tight 360 degree spin and receives a pass from the next X in line. He/she shoots quickly again. The next O in line then performs the same maneuver.

Teaching Points: Use the stick as a target for each pass. Look for openings past the goalie in order to score.

Variations: Move the passing or shooting positions.

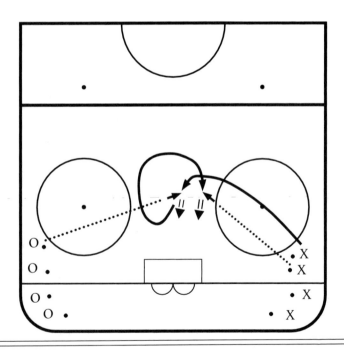

Name: Breakout Pass and Shoot Drill

Objective: To develop quick skating and shooting skills.

Age Group: Squirts and Above

Organization of Drill: Xs and Os line up in the corners as shown. The first X skates around the face-off dot with hard crossovers, then curls up the boards to receive a breakout pass from the coach. He/She then skates to the neutral zone, performs a 360 degree spin and attacks the goal. The first O then performs the same drill.

Teaching Points: Skate hard and turn as soon as possible to receive the pass.

Variations: Have a player take the place of the coach making the pass.

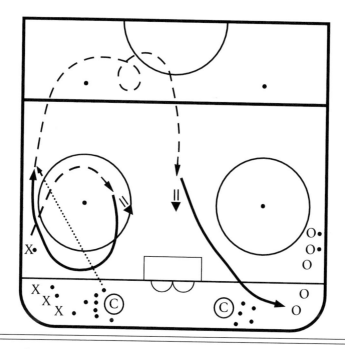

Name: Skate and Pivot Drill

Objective: To develop quick skating and shooting skills.

Age Group: Squirts and Above

Organization of Drill: Xs and Os line up at the blue line as shown. The first X skates backwards below the face-off dot and places his stick down on the ice, signifying that he/she wants a pass. The next X in line passes to X. X then skates forward up to the blue line, pivots and skates backwards to the middle of the ice, pivots again and attacks the net. The first O in line then performs the same drill.

Teaching Points: Skate backwards full speed.

Variations: Add another pass before skating across the zone.

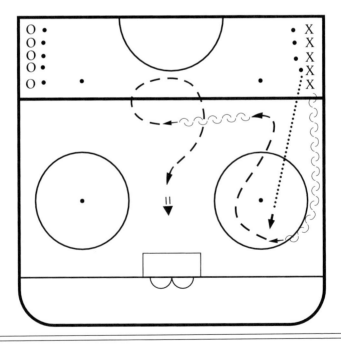

Name: Figure 8 and Shoot Drill

Objective: To develop quick skating and shooting skills.

Age Group: Squirts and Above

Organization of Drill: Xs and Os line up at the blue line as shown. The first O in line passes a puck to the first X. The first X skates a figure 8, pivoting forward and backward as shown and then attacks the net. The first O in line then performs the same drill.

Teaching Points: Perform all pivots at full speed.

Variations: Add a pass before attacking the net.

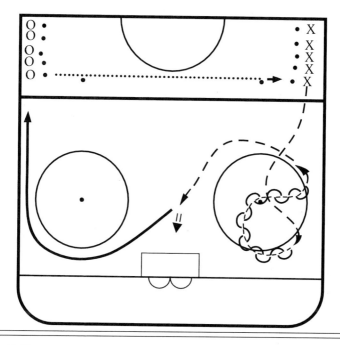

Name: Crossovers and Shoot Drill

Objective: To develop quick skating and shooting skills.

Age Group: Squirts and Above

Organization of Drill: Xs and Os line up at the blue line as shown. The first X in line skates hard into the zone and then performs crossovers back toward his/her line. At that point, the next X in line passes him/her a puck. He/She then skates to the blue line and then skates back towards the zone and attacks the net. The first O in line then performs the same drill.

Teaching Points: Skate at full speed.

Variations: Use your imagination. Add multiple tasks to the drill.

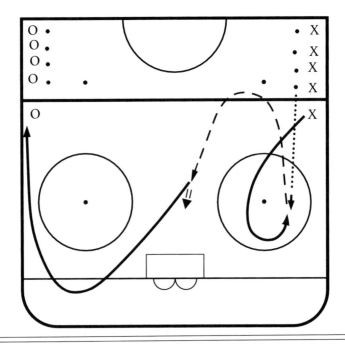

Name: Arc the Circle and Shoot Drill

Objective: To develop quick skating and shooting skills.

Age Group: Squirts and Above

Organization of Drill: Xs and Os line up in the corners as shown. The first X in line skates around the circle and receives a pass from the next X in line. He/She then skates around the neutral zone to the middle of the ice, turns and attacks the net. The first O in line then performs the same drill.

Teaching Points: Skate at full speed.

Variations: Have the second player in line make a board pass.

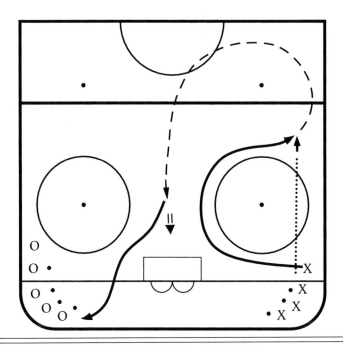

Name: Gretzky Across the Middle Drill

Objective: To develop quick skating and shooting skills.

Age Group: Squirts and Above

Organization of Drill: Line up the team as shown. The first X in line skates down and across the top of the face-off circle. He/She then skates out of the zone and receives a pass from the next player in line. He/She then skates across the zone and shoots from somewhere outside the hash marks on the other side.

Teaching Points: Skate at full speed.

Variations: Have the player perform pivots or backward skating before receiving the pass.

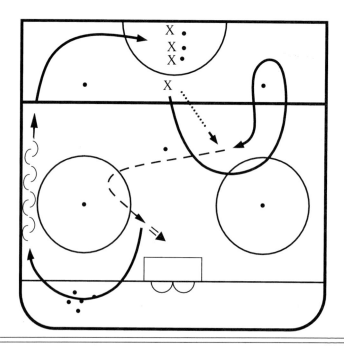

GOALTENDING DRILLS

Name: Three Shot Drill

Objective: To develop balance, movement and puck stopping skills.

Age Group: Squirts and Above

Organization of Drill: One player lines up with several pucks at positions #2 and #3; the rest of the team lines up in the #1 line. #1 starts the drill by skating out to the center line and then breaking in, taking a long shot on the goaltender. The goalie then moves to receive a shot from #2, then to #3. #2 and #3 allow the goaltender a moment to move to get set before shooting.

Teaching Points: The goaltender must try to come under control as quickly as possible to field each shot.

Variations: #2 and #3 could be allowed to take a stride in before shooting.

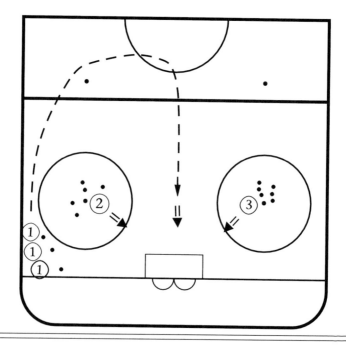

Name: Wrist Shot, Slap Shot, Deke Drill

Objective: To develop balance, movement and shot blocking skills.

Age Group: Squirts and Above

Organization of Drill: Players line up along the boards by the goal line as shown. They move as groups of three at a time. Player #1 goes around the first cone and takes a wrist shot. Player #2 skates around the second cone and takes a slap shot. Player #3 skates around the third cone and tries to deke the goalie. After the goalie is set, the next group of three begin the drill again. Players end up in the other corner and then execute the drill from the other side.

Teaching Points: Emphasize to the goalies that they must move quickly to recover from each shot and move out, cut angle and be prepared to stop the next shot.

Variations: Move the cones to different positions to create different shooting angles for the goaltender.

Name: Two Shots on the Arc Drill

Objective: To develop balance and quick recovery skills.

Age Group: Squirts and Above

Organization of Drill: Players line up in a half arc around the net as shown; each player has two pucks. On the coach's whistle, player #1 takes his/her first shot, followed as quickly as possible with his/her second shot. The goaltender is forced to react to both shots. The goaltender is allowed to receiver and then the second player in line takes his/her two shots, etc.

Teaching Points: Emphasize to the goaltender that finding the best angle will allow him/her to make the save with the least movement, better preparing him/her to stop the next shot.

Variations: For a goaltender with good skating skills, the coach could, from behind the goal, point to different players to shoot on his/her command.

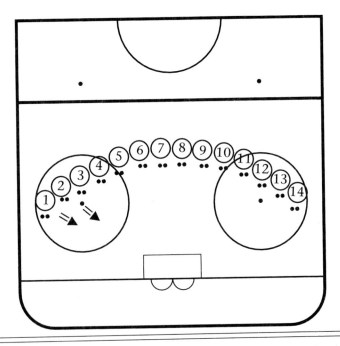

Name: V-Shot Drill

Objective: To develop balance and quick recovery skills.

Age Group: Squirts and Above

Organization of Drill: Players line up in a V as shown. Player #1 shoots, #2 gives the goaltender a moment to react, then he/she shoots. The drill continues with #3 and so on shooting on net.

Teaching Points: Emphasize to the goaltender that a good stance will provide them with the power and the quickness to get to the spot to make the next save.

Variations: For a goaltender with good skating skills, the coach could, from behind the goal, point to different players to shoot on his/her command.

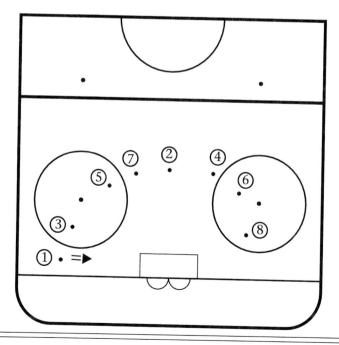

Name: Keep Up With the Shooter

Objective: To develop lateral movement and quick feet.

Age Group: Pee Wees and Above

Organization of Drill: Players line up on the face-off dots. Each player skates across the slot looking for an opening to shoot. Players alternate from each side, going back and forth. The next player should not start until the goaltender is ready for the shot.

Teaching Points: Emphasize to the goaltender that he/she needs to stay square to the shot and maintain the best angle possible. Short, quick, parallel glides are the best for this.

Variations: For a goaltenders with good skating skills, the coach could, from behind the goal, point to different players to shoot on command.

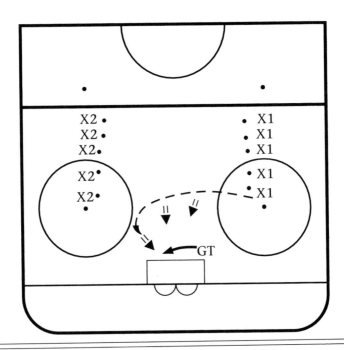

COMBINATION SKILLS
DRILLS

Name: Shoot or Pass Breaking In

Objective: To develop read and react skills and the fake shot pass technique.

Age Group: Squirts and Above

Organization of Drill: X starts with a puck and must read the goaltender. He may shoot or pass to A standing off the side of the net. X2 then performs the same drill looking to pass to B.

Teaching Points: Tell the goaltender that he/she won't have much success in this drill. Skaters must continually be reminded to try and disguise their motives.

Variations: X could pass to A or B.

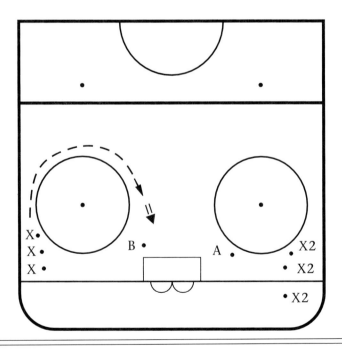

Name: Shoot or Pass

Objective: To develop read and react skills and the fake shot pass technique.

Age Group: Squirts and Above

Organization of Drill: 1 starts with a puck and passes to 2. 2 attacks the goalie and must read the goaltender. He/She may shoot or pass to 1 who has skated to the slot. 3 and 4 then perform the same drill.

Teaching Points: Tell the goaltender that he/she won't have much success in this drill. Skaters must continually be reminded to try and disguise their motives.

Variations: 2 could pass to 1 or 4 breaking to the net. Add additional tasks to the drill.

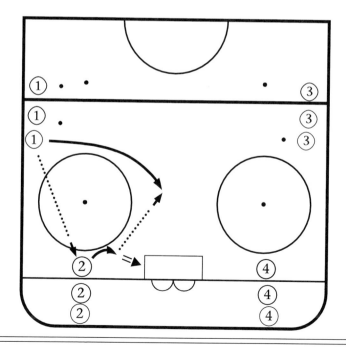

Name: Backwards/Forwards Loop With a Shot

Objective: To develop aggressive skating and shooting skills.

Age Group: Mites and Above

Organization of Drill: X starts out skating backwards and pivots at the blue line and performs hard crossovers in the neutral zone. As he/she skates towards the goal, the next player in line passes to him/her for a shot on net.

Teaching Points: Encourage the players to skate as hard as they can.

Variations: Have a coach pass the puck to each skater.

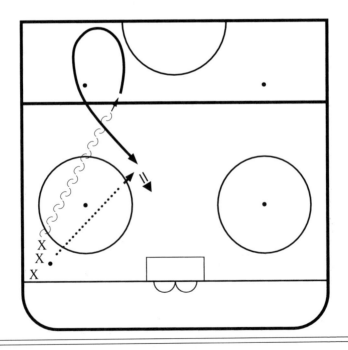

Name: Hard Crossovers and a Shot

Objective: To develop aggressive skating and shooting skills.

Age Group: Mites and Above

Organization of Drill: X starts out skating crossovers around the circle. When he/she attacks the net for a second time, the next person in line passes to them. They shoot on net.

Teaching Points: Encourage the players to skate as hard as they can.

Variations: Have a coach pass the puck to each skater.

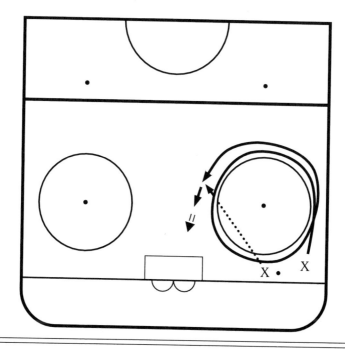

Name: Shoot and Go in the Net

Objective: To develop aggressive scoring attitudes and skills around the net.

Age Group: Mites and Above

Organization of Drill: X starts out with a puck and shoots from the top of the circle. He/She then skates hard to the net, looking for a rebound. If there is no rebound, the coach passes a puck to X for a goal mouth tip. The player can look for a rebound from that shot as well.

Teaching Points: Emphasize scoring a goal each time.

Variations: Have a player pass the puck to each shooter. Have the shooter perform a skating maneuver before going to the net for a tip.

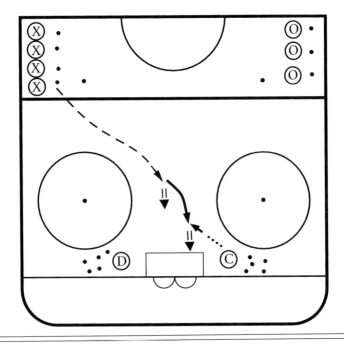

Name: 1 on 0 With a Loop

Objective: To develop aggressive skating, passing and shooting skills.

Age Group: Squirts and Above

Organization of Drill: X1 skates a loop using crossovers, skates towards X2 and receives a pass from #2; then attacks the net. #2 then performs the same drill as #1 getting a pass from the next #1 in line.

Teaching Points: Emphasize hard crossover skating, a good pass and a shot on net.

Variations: Have the players perform some other maneuver before receiving a pass, or after receiving the pass.

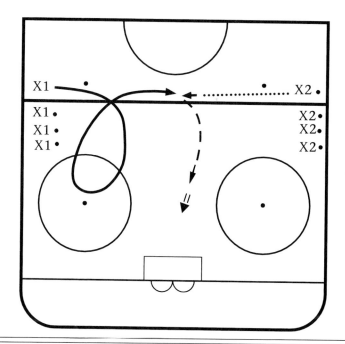

Name: Serpentine With a Shot

Objective: To develop aggressive skating and shooting skills.

Age Group: Mites and Above

Organization of Drill: X skates a serpentine route with a puck as shown, ending with a shot on net.

Teaching Points: Emphasize hard crossover skating and a shot on net.

Variations: Have the players perform some other maneuver(s). Work the drill from both sides.

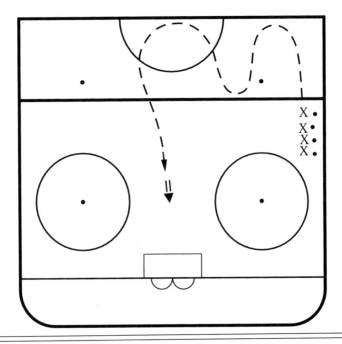

Name: Skate Three Cones

Objective: To develop aggressive skating and shooting skills.

Age Group: Mites and Above

Organization of Drill: X skates up to the blue line then around each of the cones, ending the drill with a shot.

Teaching Points: Emphasize skating and a shot on net.

Variations: Add a coach passively poke checking by any or all of the cones.

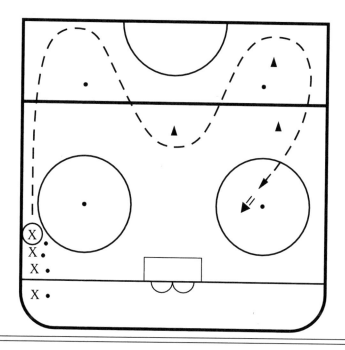

Name: Skate the Half Pretzel

Objective: To develop aggressive skating and shooting skills.

Age Group: Mites and Above

Organization of Drill: X skates around the far neutral zone faceoff dot, back under the near neutral zone faceoff dot and then circles back to attack the net.

Teaching Points: Emphasize hard crossover skating and a shot on net.

Variations: Add a coach; perform a give and go pass as the player attacks the zone.

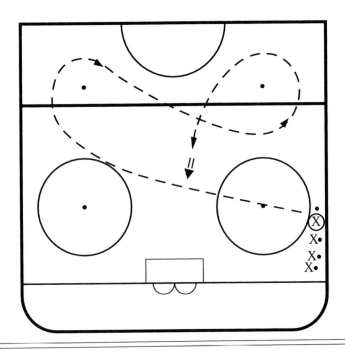

Name: 1 on 0 Pivot and Turn

Objective: To develop aggressive skating and shooting skills.

Age Group: Squirts and Above

Organization of Drill: X skates with a puck down to the bottom of the circle, pivots, and skates backwards to the blue line. At the blue line the player pivots, skates forwards along the blue line, circles the neutral zone faceoff dot and attacks the net.

Teaching Points: Emphasize hard skating and a shot on net.

Variations: Use your imagination and add additional tasks to the drill.

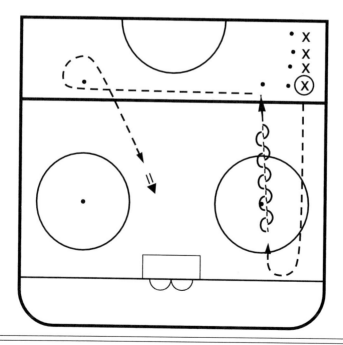

Name: Two Pass Drill

Objective: To develop aggressive skating, passing on the move and shooting skills.

Age Group: Squirts and Above

Organization of Drill: Line up players in two lines as shown. A large number of pucks need to be left behind the net. X skates around the cone and at the blue line receives a pass from the next X in line. He/She then shoots on net. He/She then circles the net, picks up a puck and passes to #2 who has timed a break to receive a pass at the top of the circle. #2 then shoots on net. X and #2 exchange lines.

Teaching Points: Emphasize hard skating, timing the break by #2, good passing and a good shot on net.

Variations: Have X skate a different route before receiving a pass.

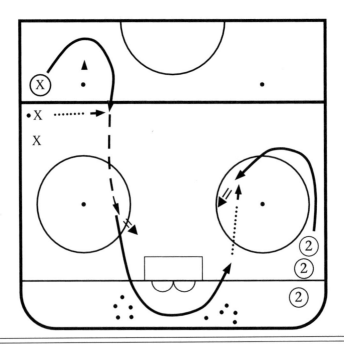

Name: Two Pass and Curl Drill

Objective: To develop aggressive skating, passing on the move and shooting skills.

Age Group: Squirts and Above

Organization of Drill: Line up players in four lines as shown. #1 skates towards line #2 and works a give and go play with the first player in line #2; then does the same with the first player in line #3. He/she then curls back towards the net for a shot. The next #3 starts the same drill with #4 and #1. Rotate lines 1-2, 2-3, 3-4, 4-1.

Teaching Points: Emphasize good passing and receiving by all players.

Variations: Start the players in different positions on the ice and use two or three pucks.

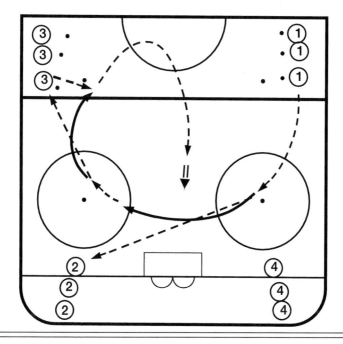

FUN DRILLS

Name: Race the Puck

Objective: To develop passing skills under pressure and aggressive skating skills.

Age Group: Squirts and Above

Organization of Drill: Line up players 1-7 as shown and a line of players where X is shown. Players #1 through #7 must complete passes to each other before X reaches the goal line on the other side.

Teaching Points: Emphasize that good execution is the key to success under pressure.

Variations: Vary the number of passers and route that X must skate.

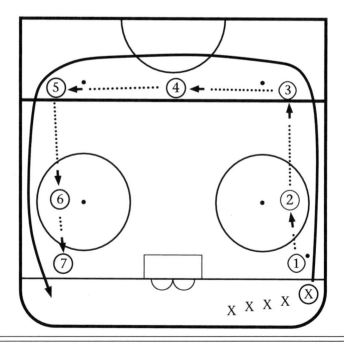

Name: Shoot and Score

Objective: To develop accurate shooting skills under pressure and aggressive skating skills.

Age Group: Mites and Above

Organization of Drill: Line up the Xs and Os as shown. On the whistle, X and O skate, then fire a shot at the side boards, bouncing it into the offensive zone. They then pick up the puck and try to shoot the puck into the net. They can not return to the line and let the next X or O go until they score. First team to score 10 goals wins.

Teaching Points: Emphasize that good execution is the key to success under pressure.

Variations: Have the skaters perform a skating maneuver before retrieving the puck off the boards.

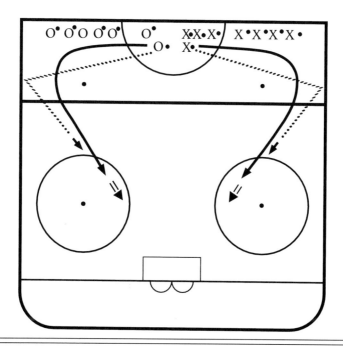

Name: 1 on 1 Battle

Objective: To develop aggressive skating and assertive 1 on 1 skills.

Age Group: Mites and Above

Organization of Drill: Line up the Xs and Os as shown. The coach dumps a puck into the zone. The first X and O in line chase down the puck and play 1 on 1, trying to score between the cones on either side of the ice.

Teaching Points: Emphasize winning the battle means working hard.

Variations: Place goaltenders in the nets. Send two players from each side in at a time.

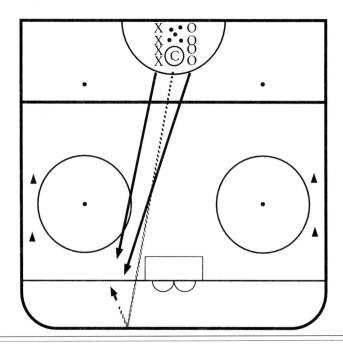

Name: Two Loop Competitive Race

Objective: To develop aggressive skating and assertive 1 on 1 skills.

Age Group: Mites and Above

Organization of Drill: Line up the Xs and Os as shown. The coach dumps a puck into the zone and the first X and O in line perform a loop first around the cone and the faceoff dot, then the second cone and the first cone, then skate to the middle looking for the puck that the coach has slid into the high slot. They play 1 on 1 until someone scores or the coach stops the play.

Teaching Points: Emphasize winning the battle means working hard.

Variations: Send two players from each line.

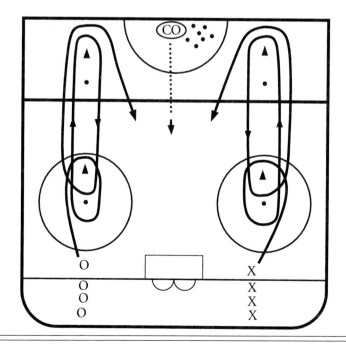

Name: Mancini Breakaway Drill

Objective: To develop breakaway and backchecking skills.

Age Group: Mites and Above

Organization of Drill: Line up the Xs on the red line and Os at the bottom of the circle. O starts with a puck and when the coach blows the whistle, O tries to score while X chases him/her down, trying to stop or hurry the shot.

Teaching Points: Emphasize winning the battle means working hard.

Variations: Start the players from a different spot.

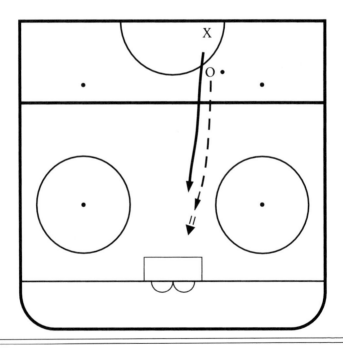

Name: Fox and Hound

Objective: To develop hard, aggressive skating skills.

Age Group: Mites and Above

Organization of Drill: Line up #1 and #2 as shown. On the whistle, #1 and #2 race around the cones trying to be the first to circle the cones twice.

Teaching Points: Emphasize skating full out and using gliding as little as possible.

Variations: Start the players from different spots. Skate in both directions.

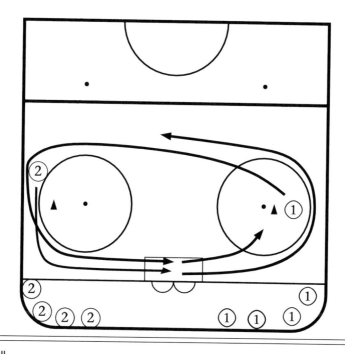

Name: Board Pass Relay

Objective: To develop board passing angles.

Age Group: Squirts and Above

Organization of Drill: Line up the Xs and Os as shown. On the whistle, the first player in each line skates up the boards making 4 board passes to him/herself. The player then races with the puck back to the line to hand off the puck to the next person in line.

Teaching Points: Emphasize selecting the best angle to use for the board pass.

Variations: Make sure all players perform this drill to the forehand and backhand sides.

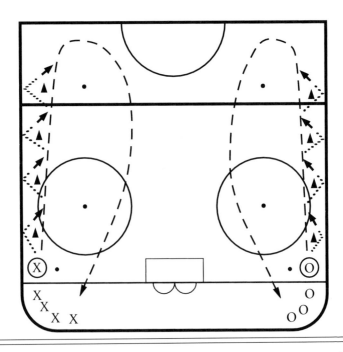

Name: Figure 8 Race

Objective: To develop competitiveness and aggressive skating skills.

Age Group: Mites and Above

Organization of Drill: Divide up your team into two groups, Xs and Os, as shown. On the whistle, the first player in each line skates a figure 8 around the cones and races to a loose puck the coach has slid into the high slot. The two players battle for the puck until one scores or the coach stops the activity.

Teaching Points: Encourage keeping the feet moving and as little gliding as possible.

Variations: Keep score and provide the winning side with a small reward or losers get a small task to do. Alter the skating route.

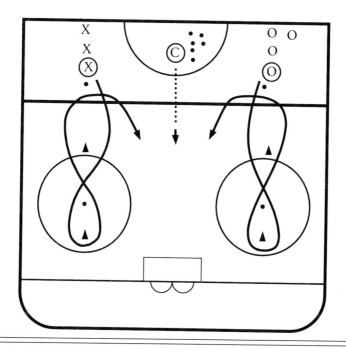

Name: Dog Sled Races

Objective: To develop strong strides, competitiveness and aggressive skating.

Age Group: Mites and Above

Organization of Drill: Divide up your team into pairs of players about the same size. O gets behind his/her partner X and gets down on his/her knees. X and O hold each other's sticks, one with each hand. X then pulls O down the ice. At the center line, O and X exchange places and return to the goal line.

Teaching Points: Encourage keeping the feet moving and as little gliding as possible.

Variations: Have two Xs pull one O. For mites, the pulled player might need to be on his/her skates, rather than on their knees.

Name: SCORO

Objective: Fun and competitiveness.

Age Group: Mites and Squirts

Organization of Drill: Divide the team into two evenly skilled groups. Line 10-20 pucks along the middle of the ice and place two net (or goals made from cones) as shown. No goaltenders are used. On the whistle, the two teams try to score goals in the other team's net. The team to have scored the most goals in the other team's net when all the pucks have been shot, wins.

Teaching Points: Encourage assertive play.

Variations: Move the nets to alternative positions, possibly back to back at center ice.

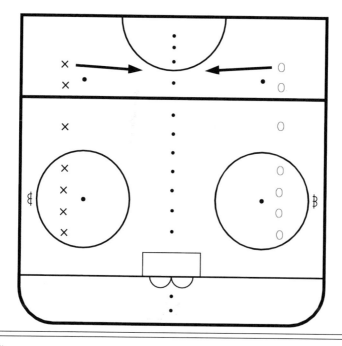

Name: Backwards Demolition Derby

Objective: Fun balance while skating backwards.

Age Group: Mites, Squirts, Pee Wees

Organization of Drill: Place five plus players in each of the end zone faceoff circles and three in the half center ice faceoff circle. On the whistle, all players must skate backward trying to knock the other players to the ice. They may not use their hands. Any player skating out of the circle is declared "out." Play until their is only one player standing in each circle.

Teaching Points: Encourage assertive play.

Variations: Use your imagination.

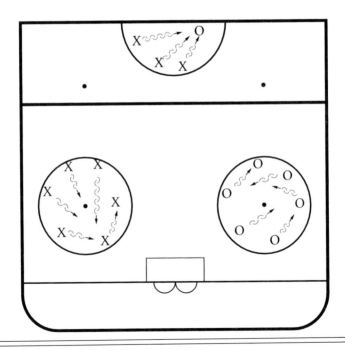

Name: Crows and Cranes

Objective: Stopping and starting skills.

Age Group: Mites, Squirts, Pee Wees

Organization of Drill: Divide the team into two teams named the "Crows" and the "Cranes." Line the players up at the inside hash marks of each circle. When the coach yells, "Crows," the crows chase and try to tag the cranes. If they do, all "tagged" cranes are out. At any time, however, the coach can yell, "cranes." This changes the drill, and signals that the crane should now chase the crows. Being "tagged" means out of the game.

Teaching Points: Encourage quick stops and starts. Have fun.

Variations: Use your imagination.

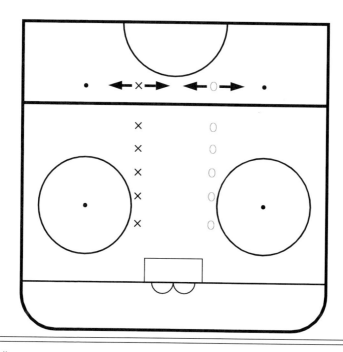

Name: Freeze Tag

Objective: To develop balance and the use of edges.

Age Group: Mites, Squirts, Pee Wees

Organization of Drill: Players spread out around the half ice area. The circled X player is "it." If the circled X tags any player, they must stop and raise their hand to signify that they have been caught. Any player can skate by and "unfreeze" them by touching them again. The play goes on until the coach assigns a new "it."

Teaching Points: Should you have a very weak player on your team, allow the player to select a helper to assist him/her. Have fun.

Variations: Move the net to the center of the zone (be careful).

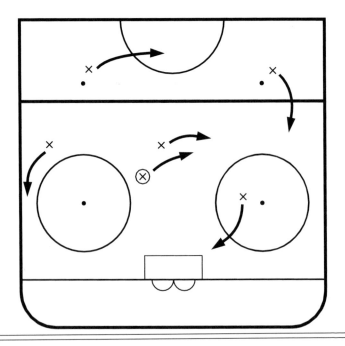

Name: Asteroids

Objective: To develop balance and the use of edges.

Age Group: Mites, Squirts, Pee Wees

Organization of Drill: Players are divided into two groups, Xs and Os. The coaches all have pucks and are positioned as shown. A coach yells, "Asteroids," and the Xs try to skate across the zone without being hit by a puck shot on the ice by the coaches, who aim for their skates. If a player is hit, he/she joins the coaches in shooting at the asteroids. The Os follow the Xs when the coach calls, "Asteroids" the second time.

Teaching Points: Players should be clearly told that there is no lifting of the puck. Have fun.

Variations: Use your imagination.

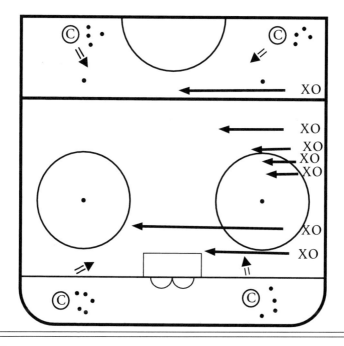

Name: 2 on 0 Race

Objective: To develop passing skills under pressure.

Age Group: Mites and Above

Organization of Drill: Players are divided into two groups, Xs and Os. Two nets and goaltenders are positioned as shown. On the whistle, the Xs and Os, in pairs, try to score on their respective nets. The pair can not return to the line and let the next group go until they have scored. Play for two to three minute intervals. Team with the most goals wins the game.

Teaching Points: Demand good passes.

Variations: Require each pair to pass the puck three times before scoring.

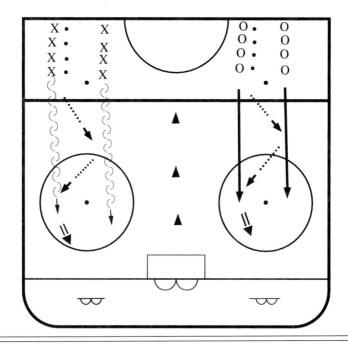

Name: 2 on 0 - Score Three Times

Objective: To develop passing skills under pressure.

Age Group: Squirts and Above

Organization of Drill: Players are divided into two groups, Xs and Os. Two nets and goaltenders are positioned as shown. Three pucks are placed on the blue line on each side of the ice. On the whistle, the Xs and Os, in pairs, try to score on their respective nets. The first pair of Xs or Os to score with all three pucks, wins. The next pair then play against each other.

Teaching Points: Demand good passes.

Variations: Require each pair to pass the puck three times before scoring.

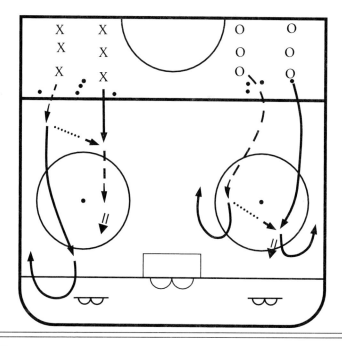

ONE ON ONE DRILLS

Name: Quick Crossunders 1 on 1 Drill

Objective: To develop quick backwards crossovers and good 1 on 1 skills for defensemen and good drive skating techniques for forwards.

Age Group: Squirts and Above

Organization of Drill: The defensemen and forwards line up as shown. The defenseman performing the drill makes a pass to the forward and makes several quick, powerful crossunders, keeping the forward to the outside. The forward wants to use drive skating and puck protection techniques to skate past the defenseman.

Teaching Points: The defensemen cannot allow the forward to gain the middle of the ice. The forward wants to drive the defenseman deep and either drive to the outside or cut back in front of the defenseman to gain the best shooting angle possible.

Variations: Work from both sides of the ice.

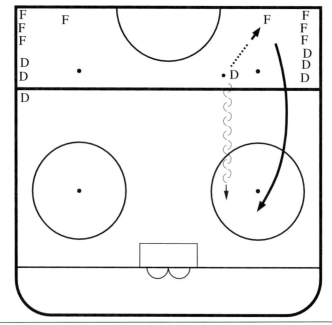

Name: 1 on 1 Quick Pivot Drill

Objective: To develop quick pivot, backwards crossovers and good 1 on 1 skills for defensemen and good skating techniques for forwards.

Age Group: Pee Wees and Above

Organization of Drill: The defenseman and forwards line up as shown. The defenseman performing the drill skates from the top of the circle to the blue line and makes a pass to the forward. He/She then makes a pivot and several quick, powerful crossunders, keeping the forward to the outside. The forward wants to use drive skating and puck protection techniques to skate past the defenseman.

Teaching Points: The defensemen cannot allow the forward to gain the middle of the ice. The forward wants to drive the defenseman deep and either drive to the outside or cut back in front of the defenseman to gain the best shooting angle.

Variations: Work from both sides of the ice.

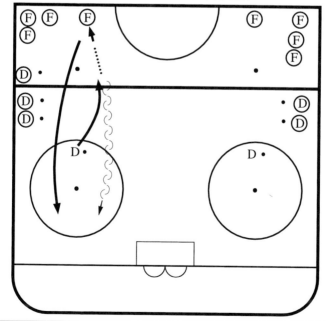

Name: 1 on 1 From the Side

Objective: To develop quick backwars skating and lateral backward crossovers for defensemen; puck control skills for forwards while performing crossovers.

Age Group: Squirts and Above

Organization of Drill: The defensemen and forwards line up as shown. The defenseman performing the drill skates backward around the cone keeping the forward to the outside. The forward wants to use good stickhandling and puck protection technique to drive past or cut back against the defenseman.

Teaching Points: The defenseman cannot allow the forward to gain the middle of the ice. The forward wants to drive the defenseman deep and either drive to the outside or cut back in front of the defenseman to gain the best shooting angel possible.

Variations: Work from both sides of the ice.

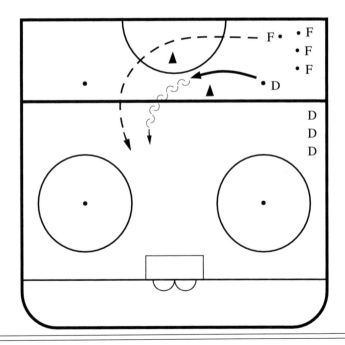

Name: 1 on 1 From the Side With a Loop

Objective: To develop quick backward skating and lateral backward crossovers for defensemen; puck control skills for forwards while performing crossovers.

Age Group: Pee Wees and Above

Organization of Drill: The defensemen and forwards line up as shown. The defenseman performing the drill skates backward around the cone keeping the forward to the outside. The forward must skate around the cone using good stickhandling and puck protection techniques to drive past or cut back against the defenseman. After each player has gone around their respective cone, the coach blows the whistle and each player must skate around the cone again, creating a new situation.

Teaching Points: The defenseman cannot allow the forward to gain the middle of the ice. The forward wants to drive the defenseman deep and either drive to the outside or cut back in front of the defenseman to gain the best shooting angle.

Variations: Work from both sides of the ice.

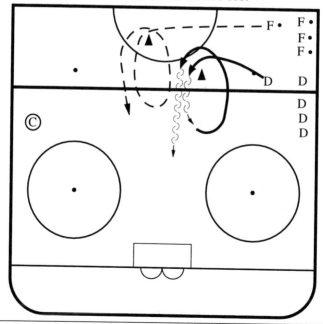

Name: 1 on 1 Circle the Cones

Objective: To develop quick pivots and backward skating for defensemen; quick skating and puck control skills for forwards while performing crossovers.

Age Group: Pee Wees and Above

Organization of Drill: The defensemen and forwards line up as shown. The defenseman and forward skate around their set of cones. The forward must then skate to the blue line and then attack. The defenseman must skate to the blue line before retreating to take the attack.

Teaching Points: The defenseman is at a real disadvantage in this drill because the forward has so much ice to use. He/ She must skate hard laterally backwards to maintain control of the forward.

Variations: Work from both sides of the ice.

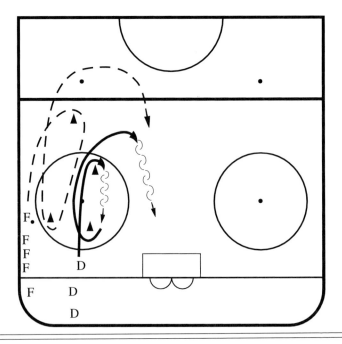

Name: 1 on 1 From a Start and Stop Drill

Objective: To develop quick pivot, backwards crossovers and good 1 on 1 skills for defensemen; stopping with the puck, and good drive skating techniques for forwards.

Age Group: Squirts and Above

Organization of Drill: The defensemen and forwards line up as shown. The defenseman passes to the forward and each skates out of the zone. When the forward reaches the cone he/she stops and attacks back into the zone. The defenseman stops when the forward stops, pivots and plays the attack back into the zone.

Teaching Points: The defenseman cannot allow the forward to gain the middle of the ice. The forward wants to drive the defenseman deep and either drive to the outside or cut back in front of the defenseman to gain the best shooting angle.

Variations: Work from both sides of the ice.

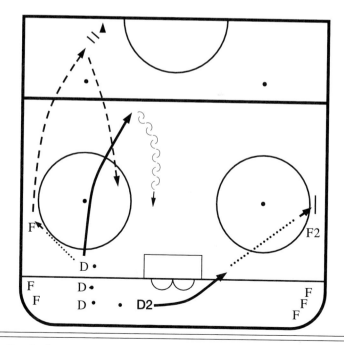

Name: 1 on 1 From Breakout Option

Objective: To develop drill on the execution of breakout options and play 1 on 1.

Age Group: Squirts and Above

Organization of Drill: The defensemen and forwards line up as shown. The defenseman reverses behind the net and immediately passes to #2 who has assumed a position along the boards. #2 skates to the blue line, then turns and attacks the zone. The defenseman skates over the blue line, then pivots and plays the 1 on 1.

Teaching Points: Watch out for slap passes. Demand quality passes every time. Encourage the players to skate at full speed.

Variations: Develop using a one or two-man breakout option.

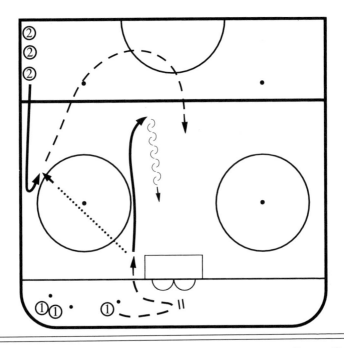

Name: 1 on 1 From a Serpentine

Objective: To develop aggressive skating and 1 on 1 play technique.

Age Group: Squirts and Above

Organization of Drill: The defensemen and forwards line up as shown. The forward skates down the blue line, power turns back to the center line then turns again and attacks the net. The defenseman pivots each time the forward turns setting him/herself to play the 1 on 1.

Teaching Points: Encourage hard, aggressive skating.

Variations: Have each player perform a loop rather than a "S" shape.

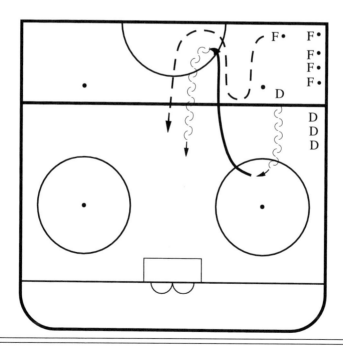

Name: 1 on 1 With a Big Loop

Objective: To develop aggressive skating and 1 on 1 play technique.

Age Group: Squirts and Above

Organization of Drill: The forward breaks across the zone and the defenseman passes him/her the puck. The forward then makes a big loop up to the red line and attacks the net. The defenseman must skate forward until the forward turns back towards the goal. He/She can then pivot and play the 1 on 1.

Teaching Points: Encourage hard, aggressive skating.

Variations: Work from both sides of the ice.

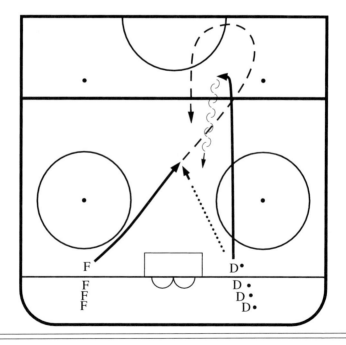

Name: 1 on 1 Serpentine with D Long Skate

Objective: To develop aggressive skating and 1 on 1 play technique.

Age Group: Squirts and Above

Organization of Drill: The forward skates a serpentine route as shown, attacking the net. The defenseman must skate from the goal line to the blue line before he/she can pivot and play the 1 on 1.

Teaching Points: Encourage hard, aggressive skating.

Variations: Work from both sides of the ice.

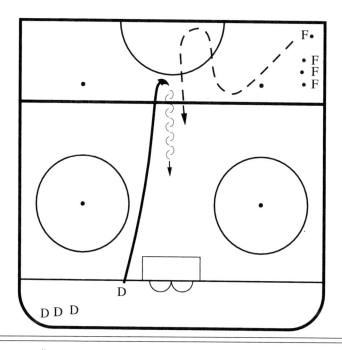

Name: 1 on 1 Blue Line In

Objective: To develop backchecking skills and 1 on 1 play technique.

Age Group: Mites and Above

Organization of Drill: #1 is the offensive player being backchecked by X. #1 can go anywhere in the zone to elude X's checking. When #1 gets free, the coach will pass him/her the puck. The play continues until the coach blows the whistle.

Teaching Points: Encourage hard, aggressive skating, tight 1 on 1 backchecking coverage and getting open for a pass.

Variations: Send in two offensive and defensive players at one time.

Name: 1 on 1 Big Arc

Objective: To develop backchecking skills and 1 on 1 play technique.

Age Group: Mites and Above

Organization of Drill: #1 is the offensive player being backchecked by X. #1 and X must skate around the two cones placed in the neutral zone; after that #1 can go anywhere in the zone to elude X's checking. When #1 gets free, the coach will pass him/her the puck. The play continues until the coach blows the whistle.

Teaching Points: Encourage hard, aggressive skating, tight 1 on 1 backchecking coverage and getting open for a pass.

Variations: Send in two offensive and defensive players at one time.

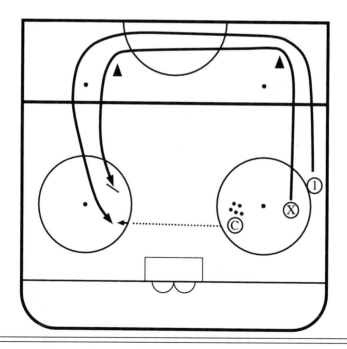

Name: Russian 1 on 1

Objective: To develop aggressive skating and 1 on 1 play technique.

Age Group: Squirts and Above

Organization of Drill: #2 starts the drill by passing to #3 as he/she breaks up the boards. #3 then skates around the cones and attacks the net. #2 must skate to the blue line, pivot and play the 1 on 1.

Teaching Points: Encourage hard, aggressive skating by both forwards and defensemen.

Variations: Use your imagination.

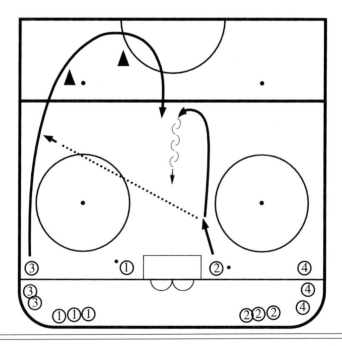

Name: 1 on 1 Angle Chaser

Objective: To develop aggressive skating, angling and check skills.

Age Group: Mites and Above

Organization of Drill: #1 starts with a puck and must skate along the boards and then around the cone, trying to get to the blue line without being checked. #2 must perform a power turn around the cone and then chase #1 trying to poke check (mites and squirts) or body check #1 (pee wee and above) before the blue line.

Teaching Points: Encourage hard, aggressive skating by both players.

Variations: Adjust the starting points to fit the skill abilities of your players.

Name: 1 on 1 Big Loop Two Cone Chaser

Objective: To develop aggressive skating, angling and check-ing skills.

Age Group: Mites and Above

Organization of Drill: #1 starts with a puck and must skate along the boards and then around the cone, trying to get to the blue line without being checked. #2 must power turn around both cones and then chase #1 trying to poke check (mites and squirts) or body check #1 (pee wee and above) before the blue line.

Teaching Points: Encourage hard, aggressive skating by both players.

Variations: Adjust the starting points to fit the skill abilities of your players.

Name: 1 on 1 Out of the Corner

Objective: To develop defenseman's ability to angle and check a player attacking out of the corner.

Age Group: Mites and Above

Organization of Drill: The defenseman lines up off the far post, while the forward linrd up at the hash marks along the boards. The forward skates around the cone and attacks the net. The defenseman must angle and force the puck carrier away from a good scoring chance.

Teaching Points: The defenseman must decide whether to force the puck carrier or play more passively and let the puck carrier come to him.

Variations: Start the defenseman on his/her knees; have them start the drill with a pass; have them skate behind the net before attacking the puck carrier.

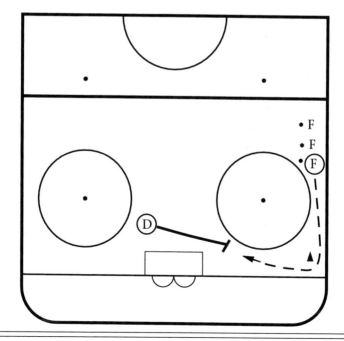

Name: 1 on 1 War

Objective: To develop confidence in competing for a loose puck.

Age Group: Mites and Above

Organization of Drill: Players X and O line up as shown. The coach slides a puck out about ten feet in front of the two players. On the whistle the two players skate to and fight for the puck trying to score a goal on that zone's net. Play continues until the coach blows his/her whistle again.

Teaching Points: Players must stay low in a good body position looking to make good shoulder to shoulder contact with the opponent.

Variations: Start the drill moving in a different direction.

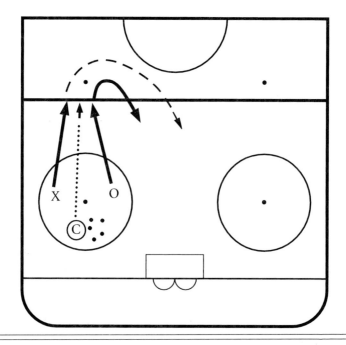

Name: 1 on 1 Across the Zone

Objective: To develop 1 on 1 offense and defensive skills.

Age Group: Mites and Above

Organization of Drill: Player X lines up on the boards and O lines up with a puck at center ice. Player O skates towards player X and passes to him/her when he/she reaches the faceoff dot. Player X then attacks across the zone while player O pivots and plays the puck carrier.

Teaching Points: Players may not move more than two stick lengths laterally during the drill.

Variations: Have O turn his/her stick around after making the pass.

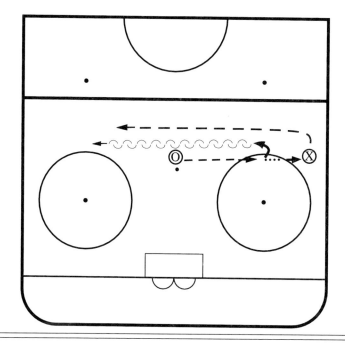

TEAM PLAY DRILLS

Name: 3 on 2 Into the Offensive Zone

Objective: To help players read and react offensively and defensively to a 3 on 2 situation.

Age Group: Squirts and Above

Organization of Drill: The players line up in position as shown. The LD starts the drill with a pass to the RW. After that, the offense and defense must read and react as the play develops.

Teaching Points: Offensive players should try to skate off the puck (get open). Defensive players should fill the middle and try to force a pass from the outside.

Variations: Have the LD pass to anyone else on the ice.

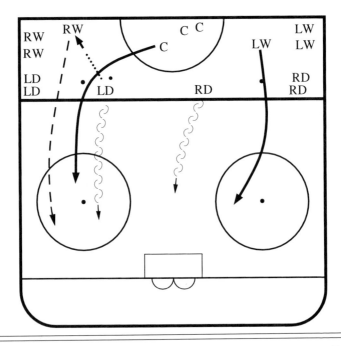

Name: 1 on 1 From a Breakout Pass

Objective: To develop breakout options and 1 on 1 skills.

Age Group: Squirts and Above

Organization of Drill: As D1 starts with the puck. F1 skates from the blue line to a breakout position. D1 passes to F1 who carries the puck, then passes to D2. D2 passes to F2 as he/she skates around the cone. D2 pivots and plays F2 in a 1/1.

Teaching Points: Emphasize good, quick passes.

Variations: Start the drill with any other breakout option you choose.

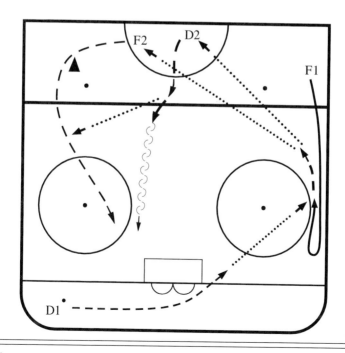

Name: 2 on 1 From a Breakout Pass

Objective: To develop breakout options and 2 on 1 skills.

Age Group: Squirts and Above

Organization of Drill: As #1 starts with puck, #2 skates from the blue line to a breakout position. #1 passes to #2 who then passes to #3 who has skated across the zone to receive the pass. #2 and #3 skate out to the center line then return and attack 2 on 1. #1 must skate up to the blue line before he/she can pivot and play the 2 on 1 back into the zone.

Teaching Points: Emphasize good, quick passes.

Variations: Start the drill with any other breakout option you choose.

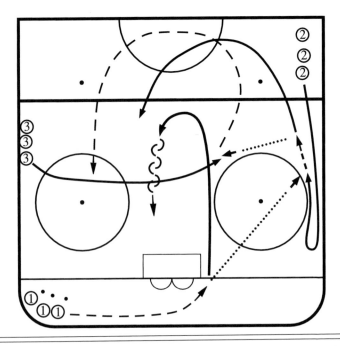

Name: 2 on 1 From a Breakout Pass

Objective: To develop breakout options and 2 on 1 skills.

Age Group: Squirts and Above

Organization of Drill: #1 starts the drill by skating towards #2 and passing to him/her, then looping around the cone back out of the zone. #2 then carries the puck around behind the net and passes to #3 who has assumed a breakout position along the boards. #3 carries the puck to the neutral zone and passes to #1. #1 and #3 attack 2 on 1 against #2.

Teaching Points: Emphasize good, quick passes. #1 must time his/her break so as not to be off-sides.

Variations: Start the drill with any other breakout option you choose.

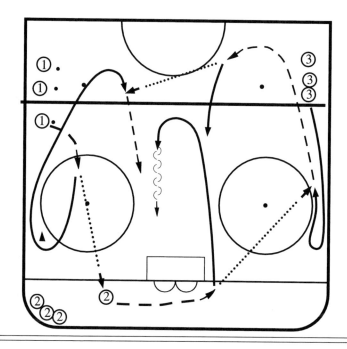

Name: 3 on 1 From a Breakout Pass

Objective: To develop breakout options and 3 on 1 skills.

Age Group: Squirts and Above

Organization of Drill: #1 starts the drill by skating towards #2 and passing to #2 who has assumed a breakout position along the boards. #2 then passes to #3 skating across the boards. #2, #3, and #4 time their attack into the offensive zone so as not to be off-sides. #1 must skate to the blue line before pivoting and playing the 3 on 1.

Teaching Points: Emphasize good, quick passes. #2 and #4 must time their breaks so as not to be off-sides.

Variations: Start the drill with any other breakout option you choose.

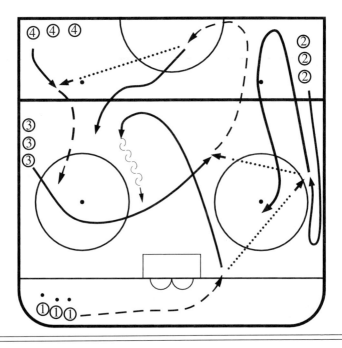

Name: 3 on 2 From a Breakout Pass

Objective: To develop breakout options and 3 on 1 skills.

Age Group: Squirts and Above

Organization of Drill: #1 starts the drill by passing to #2 who in turn passes to #3 along the boards. #3 skates towards #4 and passes to him/her. #4 attacks the zone with #5 and #6 3 on 2.

Teaching Points: Emphasize good, quick passes. #5 and #6 must time their breaks so as not to be off-sides.

Variations: Start the drill with any other breakout option you choose.

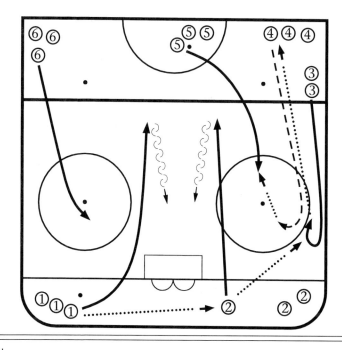

Name: 2 on 0 Regrouping Drill

Objective: To develop regrouping tactics and the basic skills needed to regroup in the neutral zone.

Age Group: Pee Wees and Above

Organization of Drill: #F1 starts the drill by passing to D1. D1 passes to D2 and they retreat passing the puck back and forth. F1 and F2 loop in the neutral zone and make themselves open for an on-sides pass from either D1 or D2, then attack the zone 2 on 0.

Teaching Points: Timing and making the stick a target for a pass are important for the forwards. Defense must move their feet and make strong, sharp passes.

Variations: Start the drill with the forwards and defensemen in slightly different positions.

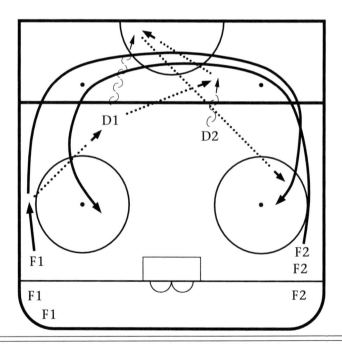

Name: 3 on 0 Regrouping Drill

Objective: To develop regrouping tactics and the basic skills needed to regroup in the neutral zone.

Age Group: Pee Wees and Above

Organization of Drill: LW starts the drill by passing to LD. LD passes to RD and they retreat passing the puck back and forth. LW, C and RW loop in the neutral zone and make themselves open for an on-sides pass from either LD or RD, then attack the zone 3 on 0.

Teaching Points: Timing (especially for the center) and making the stick a target for a pass are important for the forwards. Defense must move their feet and make strong, sharp passes.

Variations: Start the drill with the forwards and defensemen in slightly different positions.

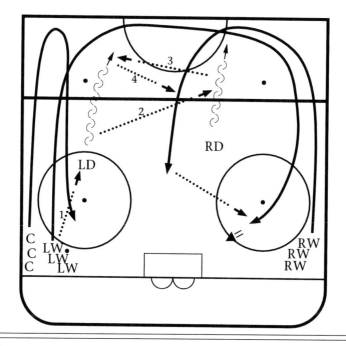

Name: Scrambled Breakout

Objective: To develop an understanding of the desired breakout positions in the defensive zone.

Age Group: Squirts and Above

Organization of Drill: A forward line (C, LW, RW) and a defensive pair (LD, RD) pass a puck around the neutral zone while skating. On the whistle, whoever has the puck dumps it into the defensive zone. The five players react to wherever the puck is and assume the appropriate breakout positions, reacting to each pass.

Teaching Points: Players should move to their spots as quickly as possible and anticipate a pass.

Variations: Send in one or two forecheckers (passively or aggressively forechecking).

Name: Defensive Zone Coverage Reaction Drill

Objective: To develop an understanding of the desired defensive zone coverages to implement.

Age Group: Squirts and Above

Organization of Drill: A forward line (C, LW, RW) and a defensive pair (LD, RD) line up at the center line. The coach passes a puck to another coach in one of the corners. Players skate to the appropriate positions to cover defensively. The coach now passes a puck to a coach (or player) somewhere else in the zone. The five defensive players react and stop in the appropriate position. The coach can continue this until he/she is satisfied the players understand the defensive zone coverage.

Teaching Points: Diagram the desired defensive zone coverages in advance (ideally off ice). Show the players the desired reactions in the zone. Correct players as needed.

Variations: Dump a puck in with several players trying to score.

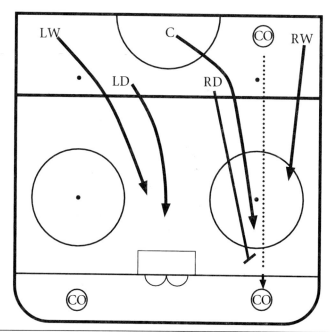

Name: 5 on 3 Down Low or 5 on 4 Down Low (depending upon the type of low zone coverage desired). 5 on 3 is shown here.

Objective: To develop an understanding of the interactions between the forwards.

Age Group: Squirts and Above

Organization of Drill: A forward line (C, LW, RW) and a defensive pair (LD, RD) line up at the center line. A defensive pair (D1, D2) and a forward (C) line up at the blue line. The coach dumps a puck in and the five man unit tries to score on the two man unit playing defense.

Teaching Points: D1, D2 and C only defend below the circles; they do not defend against the point men. The point men can only pass or shoot; they can not move closer to the goal.

Variations: Have the defending team turn their sticks around.

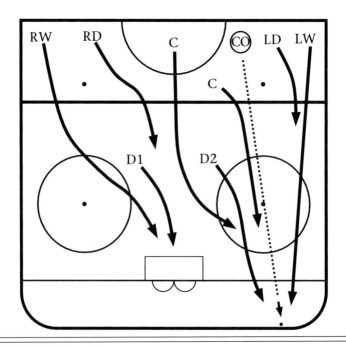

Name: 2 on 0 With Follow

Objective: To get players to continue the play after an initial shot on net.

Age Group: Squirts and Above

Organization of Drill: #1 and #2 line up as shown; #2s have a puck. The first #1 breaks around the cone and receives a pass form #2 (on-sides). The two players attack the goal 2 on 0 with an offensive play. After a shot is taken, the shooter (shown as #2) goes to the corner, picks up a puck and passes to #1 who has skated around a cone and moved to the slot. #1 shoots and the next pair of players continue the drill.

Teaching Points: The pass to #1 must be on-sides.

Variations: Call for any offensive zone rush to be executed.

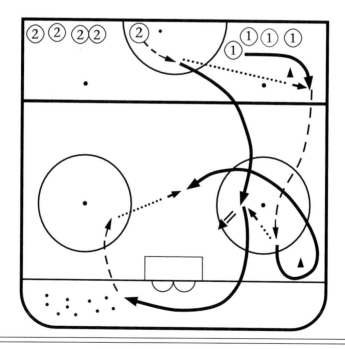

Name: 3 on 3 Cross Ice Game

Objective: To develop read and react skills.

Age Group: Squirts and Above

Organization of Drill: Two teams play against each other 3 on 3; goals are set along the side boards. Once a team gains control of the puck, they must make two passes before they can score.

Teaching Points: At first, players will want to rush towards the opponent's net to find that they have to make a pass, yet no one is open. Encourage players to develop length and width to their attack.

Variations: Play 2 on 2 and set the rule that a team, once gaining control of the puck, must pass to a coach before they can score.

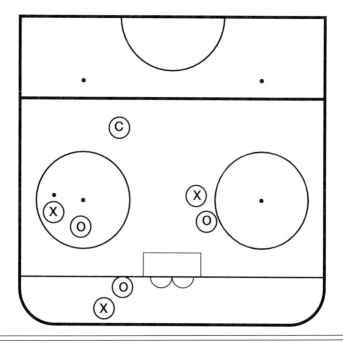

Name: 5 on 2 in the Offensive Zone

Objective: To develop offensive zone patterns as well as read and react skills.

Age Group: Squirts and Above

Organization of Drill: Organize a five man unit to play offense against two defenders (identified as X). The whistle starts play and the offensive team tries to score. The defenders can chase anywhere, and do not assume specific defensive positions. Keep score of how m any goals can be scored in one minute.

Teaching Points: This drill is a test of read and react skills. There will be openings that the players must be encouraged to find.

Variations: Add a third defender. Do not allow the defenders to use their sticks (or have them turn their sticks around).

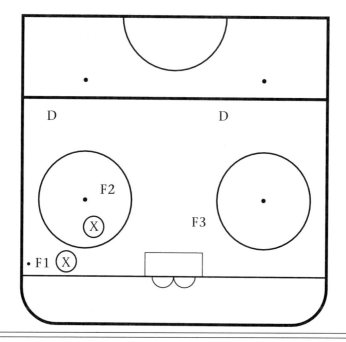

Name: Breakout to a Drop Pass

Objective: To develop breakout patterns and passing skills.

Age Group: Squirts and Above

Organization of Drill: Line up the players as shown. D1 flips a puck to the corner and then retrieves it and makes a board pass to D2. D2 passes to F1 who has timed a break across the zone. F1 then makes a drop pass for F2. They both skate around the cones respectively and they attack the net 2 on 0.

Teaching Points: Make good passes; time your breaks.

Variations: Reposition the cones that the forwards skate around. Have the defensemen perform a different breakout option.

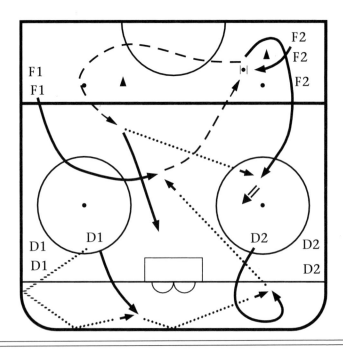

Name: Quick 2 on 0

Objective: To develop passing skills and quick decision making when on the attack.

Age Group: Squirts and Above

Organization of Drill: Line up the players as shown. X with a puck carries the puck and then passes to O. O gives X a return pass and X decides to shoot on net or pass back to O who has followed the attack.

Teaching Points: Make good passes, time your breaks.

Variations: Position O in a different spot. Work the drill from both sides of the ice.

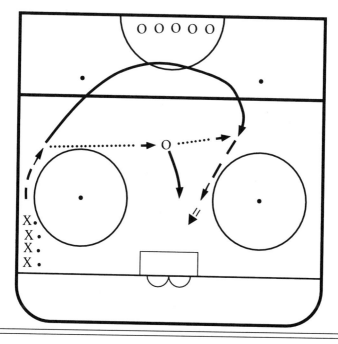

Name: Time the Pass

Objective: To develop the timing necessary to be an effective passer and receiver.

Age Group: Squirts and Above

Organization of Drill: Line up the players as shown with X1 lined up on the hash marks. X1 skates across the slot area above the dot, while X2 follows. After clearing the net X2 passes to X1 who performs a hard crossover the neutral zone and turns back attacking the net. X2 continues skating, arcs back towards the net and times a break with O who will pass to him as X2 did to X1.

Teaching Points: Make good passes, time your breaks. Be sure to let the player shooting clear the zone before you make your break.

Variations: Use your imagination.

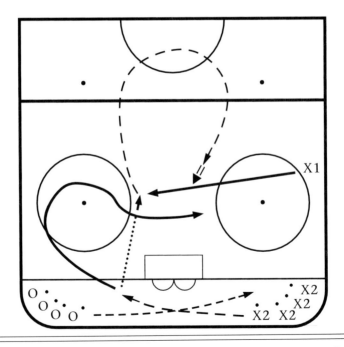

Name: One Man Regroup Drill

Objective: To develop regrouping skills and the timing necessary to this tactic.

Age Group: Squirts and Above

Organization of Drill: Line up the players as shown with Xs all having pucks. The first X carries the puck and passes to D who starts skating backwards as X skates towards him/her. D continues to carry the puck backwards as X loops around him/her, creating a good passing angle to receive a pass from D. X then shoots on net.

Teaching Points: Make good passes, time your breaks. Be sure to let the player shooting clear the zone before you make your break. Work from both sides of the ice.

Variations: Add a second and third puck.

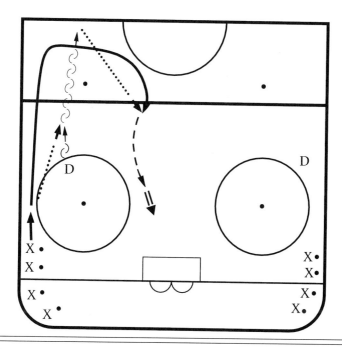

Name: 2 on 0 With Point Shots

Objective: To develop offensive skills and encourage continuation of the attack after a shot.

Age Group: Squirts and Above

Organization of Drill: Line up the players as shown. #1 and #2 start out an attack by looping into the neutral zone, then attacking the net. #1 carries the puck into the attack zone. After the rush, the defensemen who were lined up in the neutral zone move to the blue line. #1 retrieves a puck and passes to one of the defensemen. #2 goes to the net to tip and screen the goaltender. #2 then retrieves a puck and passes to the other defensemen while #1 goes to the net to tip and screen the goaltender.

Teaching Points: Good passes are critical to the success of this drill.

Variations: Allow the defensemen to move in from the point as a fourth attacker might.

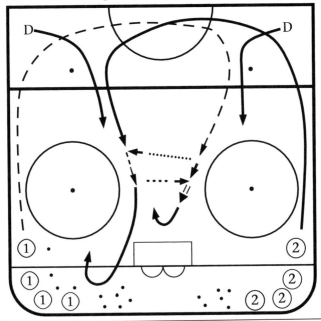

Name: Quick 2 on 1 Drill

Objective: To develop offensive skills; read and react skills.

Age Group: Squirts and Above

Organization of Drill: Line up the players as shown. #1 passes to D (defenseman) as #2 skates around him/her as well. As #1 and #2 arc towards the offensive zone, D passes to either #1 or #2, pivots and plays their rush 2 on 1.

Teaching Points: The offensive players must stay on sides and read the play.

Variations: Position the defensemen or forwards differently.

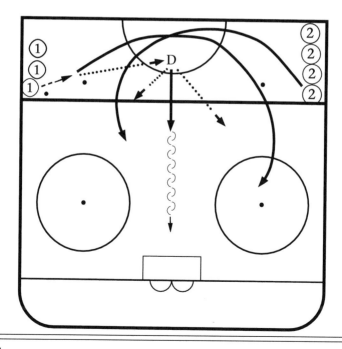

Name: Half Ice Regroup Drill

Objective: To develop regrouping and timing skills.

Age Group: Squirts and Above

Organization of Drill: F passes to D1 who retreats with the puck and passes to D2. While this happens, F loops in front of D1 and D2 and receives a pass from D2. He/she then turns back towards the net for a shot on goal. F2 would then start the same drill from the other side.

Teaching Points: The forwards in each line must provide a good target with their stick and make themselves available for the pass from the defenseman.

Variations: Add a forward on the other side and attack 2 on 0. Add a defenseman and create a 2 on 1 play.

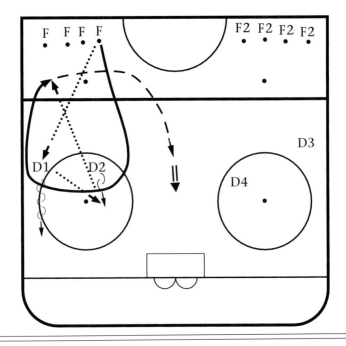

Name: Quick Give and Go Drill

Objective: To develop quick read and react skills.

Age Group: Squirts and Above

Organization of Drill: The Xs and Os are lined up as shown. (Notice that the Os are positioned ahead of the Xs). O and X break at the same time. X takes a stride and passes immediately to O (do not consider off-sides). O looks for and passes quickly back to X who shoots; O skating for a rebound.

Teaching Points: Look before making the back pass. Pass to the stick of the trailer.

Variations: Start from another position in the neutral zone.

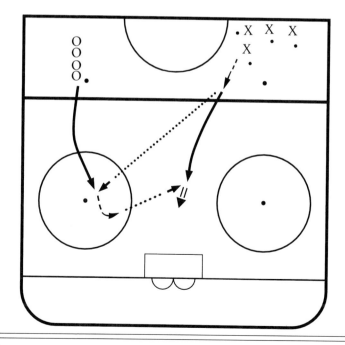

Name: Rap Pass and Shoot

Objective: To improve board passing and receiving skills.

Age Group: Squirts and Above

Organization of Drill: The Xs and Os are lined up as shown. O and X break at the same time. X takes a stride and passes immediately to O along the boards. O skates around the top of the circle and attacks the net. The next O in line then makes the same pass to the X who started the drill.

Teaching Points: Touch is important in board passing. The stick must be pressed firmly against the boards when receiving a board pass.

Variations: Use your imagination. Have multiple tasks.

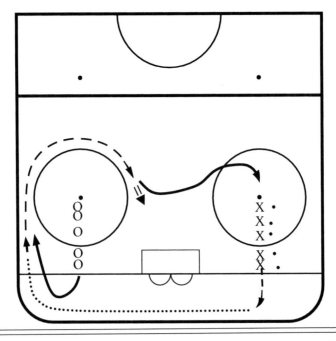

Name: Long Pass Arc and Shoot Drill

Objective: To improve passing and receiving skills.

Age Group: Squirts and Above

Organization of Drill: The Xs and Os are lined up as shown. O makes a cross ice pass to X then arcs to the center line, then back towards the end zone. X return passes to O before the blue line. O attacks the net. X then starts the drill again with a pass to the next O. X and O exchange lines picking up a puck in the opposite corner.

Teaching Points: Long passes have to be firm.

Variations: Move the players closer together for players with less skill.

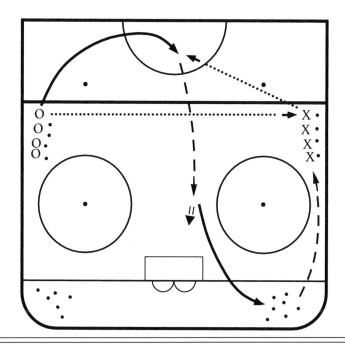

Name: Crash the Net

Objective: To improve scoring skills in the slot area.

Age Group: Squirts and Above

Organization of Drill: The two forwards skate to the front of the net to screen the goaltender after one of them passes a puck to the point (D). Two Xs (defenders) try to move them out of the slot area so that the goaltender can see the point shot.

Teaching Points: Forwards should try to keep their stick on the ice as they face the shooter. This way they will have more stability in front of the net.

Variations: Have the forwards and defenders perform a skating maneuver before skating to the front of the net.

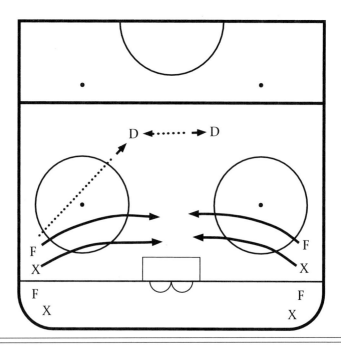

Name: 2 on 0 From a Drop Pass

Objective: To improve offensive attack skills.

Age Group: Squirts and Above

Organization of Drill: The Xs and Os are lined up as shown. X and O skate towards each other, with O leaving a drop pass for X. X drives deep in the zone as O performs a loop. X passes to O; O shoots or passes back to X for a goal mouth shot on net.

Teaching Points: X must time his/her skate, while O needs to skate hard to time his/her movement with X.

Variations: Have the forwards and defenders perform a skating maneuver before skating to the front of the net.

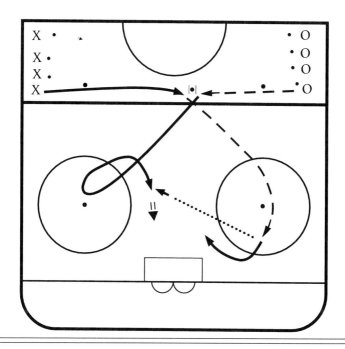

Name: 3 on 0 From Coach Pass

Objective: To improve offensive attack, along with read and react skills.

Age Group: Squirts and Above

Organization of Drill: #1, #2, and #3 are attackers lined up at the center line. The Xs are defenders lined up at the top of the circles. The attacker and defenders all start moving at the same time. The attackers move in an organized way towards the zone. The coach passes a puck to one of the attackers. The defenders must skate to the blue line, then they can begin their defense of the net. Continue the play until someone scores or the play breaks down.

Teaching Points: Emphasize the attackers to observe what the defenders are doing and to act accordingly.

Variations: Have the defenders start on their stomachs.

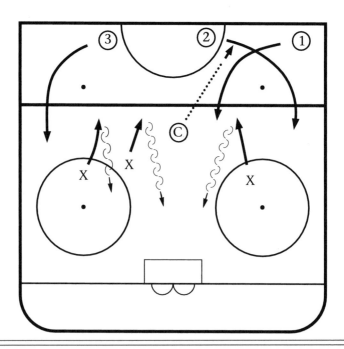

Name: 2 on 0 From Circle Drop Pass

Objective: To improve offensive attack, along with read and react skills.

Age Group: Squirts and Above

Organization of Drill: The Xs and Os are lined up as shown. O starts with a puck and skates to the top of the end zone circle; X without a puck does the same. O drop passes to X. They skate to the bottom of the circle then exchange passes in the neutral zone then attack back into the end zone, 2 on 0.

Teaching Points: Remind the player making the drop pass to leave it on the stick side of the receiver.

Variations: Have X and O perform another drop pass in the neutral zone before attacking the net.

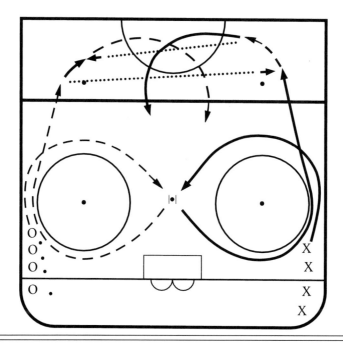

Name: 2 on 1 From a Loop

Objective: To improve offensive attack, along with read and react skills.

Age Group: Pee Wees and Above

Organization of Drill: Lines for F1, F2 and D (defensemen) as shown. F2 starts the drill by skating towards D and then passing to him/her. The D gives F2 a return pass as he/she curls across the zone. D then skates beyond the blue line, pivots and plays the rush back towards the net. F1 starts when F2 does and receives a pass from F2 in the neutral zone. F1 and F2 curl back towards the goal and attack 2 on 1.

Teaching Points: Timing the breaks is important for the play to be successful.

Variations: Start the drill from the other side.

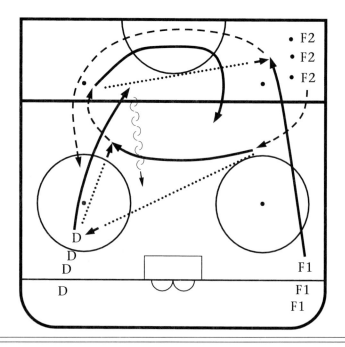

Name: 2 on 0 From a Regroup

Objective: To improve regrouping skills.

Age Group: Pee Wees and Above

Organization of Drill: #1s with a puck, #2s and two defensemen are positioned as shown. #1 and #2 skate out of the zone. #1 passes to D1. D1 then passes to D2 who then passes to #2. #2 can shoot or pass to #1 for a shot on net.

Teaching Points: #1 and #2 want to time their breaks so as to attack the zone with speed.

Variations: Use your imagination.

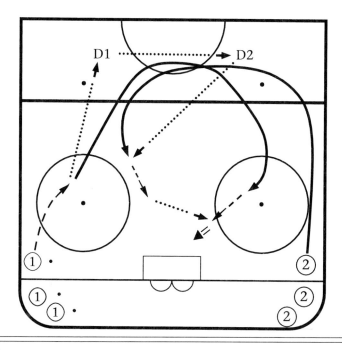

Name: 2 on 2 Half Ice Drill

Objective: To improve attack skills.

Age Group: Pee Wees and Above

Organization of Drill: F1, F2, D1 and D2 line up as shown. F1 starts the drill by passing to D1 who retreats with the puck and passes to D2. D2 passes to F2 skating across the middle. F2 then carries the puck out of the zone, then turns back towards F1. F1 breaks towards the zone and receives a pass from F2 and they attack 2 on 2. After D2 makes his/her pass, D1 and D2 must skate over the blue line before playing the attack.

Teaching Points: Timing breaks and passes are critical to successful attack. Players should be skating at full speed.

Variations: When introducing the drill, do not play the drill 2 on 2. Instead, play the drill 2 on 0 so the forwards can get used to skating the drill at high speed before having to be concerned about defenders.

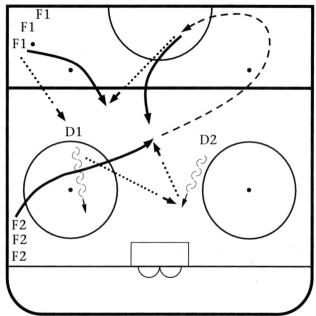